C VERSION

The
STANDARDS
REAL BOOK

A Collection Of Some Of
The Greatest Songs Of the 20th Century

Created by Musicians, for Musicians

Publisher and Editor · *Chuck Sher*
Musical Editor · *Larry Dunlap*
Music Copying · *Mansfield Music Graphics and Ann Krinitsky, Berkeley, CA*
Cover artwork · *Mosaic by Sueann Bettison-Sher*
Cover Design · *Attila A. Nagy, Cotati, CA*

STANDARD SONGS

STANDARD SONGS (Continued)

This Heart Of Mine
This Is Always
Thou Swell
Time After Time
A Time For Love
Time On My Hands
'Tis Autumn
Too Marvelous For Words
Trouble Is A Man
Twilight World

Two For The Road
Until The Real Thing Comes Along
What Is This Thing Called Love?
When The World Was Young
When Your Lover Has Gone
Where Or When?
Who Cares?
Why Try To Change Me Now?
With A Song In My Heart
You And The Night And The Music

You Are Too Beautiful
You Do Something To Me
You Go To My Head
You Make Me Feel So Young
You Taught My Heart To Sing
You Took Advantage Of Me
You'd Be So Nice To Come Home To
You'll Never Know
You're The Top
Yours Is My Heart Alone

POP STANDARDS

AL JARREAU
I Will Be Here For You
Love Speaks Louder Than Words
Not Like This
We're In This Love Together

DIONNE WARWICK
Close To You
I Say A Little Prayer For You
That's What Friends Are For
Walk On By
What The World Needs Now Is Love

BRENDA RUSSELL
Get Here
Piano In The Dark

DAVE SANBORN
As We Speak

THE DOOBIE BROTHERS
Minute By Minute
Real Love
Taking It To The Streets
What A Fool Believes

LIONEL RICHIE
Hello
Stuck On You

GEORGE BENSON
Everything Must Change
Valdez In The Country

CHAKA KHAN
Through The Fire

TOM SCOTT
Sure Enough

MISCELLANEOUS POP
Ain't No Sunshine
Caught Up In The Rapture
The Dock Of The Bay
Don't Be Blue
In The Midnight Hour
Moondance
One Hundred Ways
Pick Up The Pieces
People Make The World Go 'Round
Saving All My Love For You
Something To Talk About
A Song For You
Soul Man
Suite: Judy Blue Eyes
Sunny
Until It's Time For You To Go
When A Man Loves A Woman
You Make Me Feel Brand New

JAZZ STANDARDS

DUKE ELLINGTON
Cottontail
I Didn't Know About You
Rockin' In Rhythm
What Am I Here For?

HORACE SILVER
Doodlin'
Tokyo Blues
Too Much Saké

DAVE FRISHBERG
The Underdog
Wheelers And Dealers
You Are There

ANTONIO CARLOS JOBIM
Agua De Beber
A Felicidade
The Girl From Ipanema
How Insensitive
Meditation
Sabia

MILES DAVIS
'Round Midnight
Walkin'

COUNT BASIE
Blue And Sentimental
Lester Leaps In

MISCELLANEOUS JAZZ
Bags' Groove
Bluesette
Doxy
Forest Flower
The Old Country
Red Clay
Take Five
Those Eyes

TADD DAMERON
Good Bait
Hot House
On A Misty Night
Our Delight

Alphabetical Index

Composition	Composed by/As Played by	Page

Index of Standard Songs by Major Composers

GEORGE & IRA GERSHWIN
Bess, You Is My Woman
Bidin' My Time
But Not For Me
Embraceable You
Fascinating Rhythm
A Foggy Day
How Long Has This Been Going On?
I Got Rhythm
I Loves You Porgy
I Was Doing All Right
I've Got A Crush On You
Isn't It A Pity
It Ain't Necessarily So
Let's Call The Whole Thing Off
Love Walked In
The Man I Love
My Man's Gone Now
Nice Work If You Can Get It
Of Thee I Sing
Oh, Lady Be Good
(Our) Love Is Here To Stay
'S Wonderful
Somebody Loves Me
Someone To Watch Over Me
Soon
Strike Up The Band
Summertime
That Certain Feeling
They All Laughed
They Can't Take That Away From Me
Thou Swell
Who Cares?

HARRY WARREN
At Last
I Had The Craziest Dream
I Only Have Eyes For You
I Wish I Knew
Lullaby Of Broadway
The More I See You
September In The Rain
Serenade In Blue
Summer Night
This Heart Of Mine
This Is Always
You'll Never Know

SAMMY FAIN
Alice In Wonderland
Love Is A Many Splendored Thing
Secret Love

COLE PORTER
After You
All Of You
All Through The Night
Anything Goes
At Long Last Love
Begin The Beguine
Dream Dancing
Easy To Love
From This Moment On
Get Out Of Town
I Concentrate On You
I Get A Kick Out Of You
I Love Paris
I Love You
I've Got You Under My Skin
It's All Right With Me
It's De-Lovely
Just One Of Those Things
Let's Do It
Love For Sale
Miss Otis Regrets
Night And Day
So In Love
What Is This Thing Called Love?
You Do Something To Me
You'd Be So Nice To Come Home To
You're The Top

HAROLD ARLEN
Blues In The Night
I Gotta Right To Sing The Blues
Stormy Weather

JOHNNY MANDEL
Close Enough For Love
A Time For Love
You Are There

MICHEL LEGRAND
How Do You Keep The Music Playing?
I Will Wait For You
The Summer Knows

CY COLEMAN
The Best Is Yet To Come
I'm Gonna Laugh You Right Out Of My Life
Why Try To Change Me Now?

ALEC WILDER
Blackberry Winter
Trouble Is A Man

RODGERS & HART
Bewitched
Blue Room
Dancing On The Ceiling
Falling In Love With Love
Have You Met Miss Jones?
He Was Too Good To Me
I Could Write A Book
I Didn't Know What Time It Was
I Wish I Were In Love Again
It Never Entered My Mind
Johnny One Note
The Lady Is A Tramp
Mountain Greenery
My Funny Valentine
My Heart Stood Still
There's A Small Hotel
Where Or When
With A Song In My Heart
You Are Too Beautiful
You Took Advantage Of Me

HENRY MANCINI
Charade
Days Of Wine And Roses
Dreamsville
Mr. Lucky
Slow Hot Wind
Two For The Road

DIETZ & SCHWARTZ
Alone Together
Dancing In The Dark
I Guess I'll Have To Change My Plan
If There Is Someone Lovelier Than You
You And The Night And The Music

CAHN & STYNE
The Christmas Waltz
It's Magic
It's You Or No One
Time After Time

JIMMY VAN HEUSEN
All My Tomorrows
All The Way
Come Fly With Me
Nancy (With The Laughing Face)

LEONARD BERNSTEIN
Lucky To Be Me
Some Other Time

Publisher's Foreword

We at Sher Music Co. are again proud to present to you a compilation of some of the greatest songs ever written, this time all standards in one way or another. We hope and know that you will find this volume to be of much use in your pursuit of beauty and we have taken every measure possible to insure that each tune is presented accurately.

For the Standard Songs (the great bulk of the book), we have used many of the best jazz and jazz vocal versions to arrive at a consensus of how the tune has been interpreted over the years. What you get here is much more than just a reprint of the original sheet music—it is a distilled version of how each tune has evolved, with the best and/or most common chord changes included.

Main And Alternate Chords

Our basic goal was to have the bottom, or main changes reflect the common practice of how a jazz player would be expected to play the tune on a gig or at a jam session. You can feel confident calling any of the standards in this book and telling your bandmates to use the bottom changes—they should sound just right in every case. The alternate chords above the main chords have several different functions. Sometimes they are hipper substitute chords, often classic ones used by Miles Davis, Bill Evans, Coltrane, etc. On other occasions, the alternate chords are a reflection of the earlier Broadway or cabaret-style changes found in the original sheet music. Sometimes the alternate changes are a simpler version of the main changes, to be used during solo choruses. We suggest that you read through the alternate changes on any given tune before performing them to see if, or in what way, you want to incorporate them into your version of the tune.

Transcription Choices

For some of the Standard Songs we have included direct transcriptions of the greatest jazz versions of the song, either as the only chart included (e.g. Bill Evans' "My Man's Gone Now" and "Alice In Wonderland") or as separate alternate versions (e.g. Coltrane's "But Not For Me"), or sometimes both, e.g. the standard version of "Summertime" followed on page 2 of the chart by Miles & Gil Evans' classic version. We hope you enjoy seeing these "Great Moments In Jazz" put down on paper for you to work off of.

The Jazz Standards and the Pop Standards are usually direct transcriptions of the original version of the tune, often with added features such as separate rhythm section parts (e.g. "What A Fool Believes"). In general, we have tried to format the charts in this book so that they could be played on a gig without rehearsal, but for many of the more contemporary pop standards we decided that more involved charts were essential to capture the beauty of the original recording.

By design, this book is full of tunes that you and your audiences know and love. The few more obscure tunes were included because they were just too beautiful to omit. So do yourself a favor and play through the tunes you might not have heard of (e.g. "Not Like This", "Those Eyes" and "I Have The Feeling I've Been Here Before".) You'll be glad you did.

Thank Yous

All of us who will be using this book for many years to come owe Dave Olsen of Warner Brothers Publications in Miami a big "Thank You!". Being a musician himself, Dave understood the artistic and historical significance of this project and was instrumental in helping Sher Music Co. obtain permission to use most of the tunes in this book. It simply wouldn't have happened without him. Thanks, big guy! And thanks too to the rest of the good people at Warner Bros., especially Cheryl Swack, who helped make this particular dream a reality.

I personally owe a big debt of gratitude to Larry Dunlap who devoted every spare minute for about a year to getting this book transcribed and for doing a world-class job. But what else would you expect from a world-class pianist, arranger and all-around professional? Also, thanks to Mark Levine (the one and only) who proofread these charts and made numerous invaluable suggestions. In addition, thanks to Art Khu, Bob Franks, Fred Zimmerman, Will Johnson, Randy Vincent, Ray Scott, Chuck Gee and other Bay Area musicians for reading through these tunes with a critical eye. Once again, thanks are due to Ernie Mansfield and Ann Krinitsky for producing the world's most legible music manuscript, Kendrick Freeman for his careful work on the Drum Appendix and Attila Nagy for the cover design. Also, thanks to John Brenes, singer Liz Lewis, Kyle St. John, Tom Edwards and disc jockey *extraordinaire* Bob Parlocha for suggesting tunes and versions of tunes to use.

A continuous thank you to Gayle Levin, Helaine Dorenfeld, Anita Pilkington, Sue Claxton, Susan McNutt, Tom Carlin of Ag Press, and especially Ann Hyland for keeping Sher Music Co. running smoothly. And, of course, much thanks to my family—my father Maury, my brother Jon, my wonderful kids Ben and Anna, and my sweet wife, Sueann—for all the love, support, friendship and inspiration a person could ask for. (Sueann also created the gorgeous mosaic gracing the front cover of the book!) We all hope the end result will keep you smiling for years to come.

Dedication

Lastly, I would like to dedicate this book to the memory of Sky Evergreen (aka Bob Bauer) who died of AIDS in 1997. Sky was Sher Music Co.'s transcriber from our first book onwards and was wise beyond his years and musically gifted beyond the norm. We who knew him will never forget his beautiful spirit and genius.

Chuck Sher

Musical Editor's Foreword

This is a remarkable book and it once again reflects Chuck Sher's expansive vision when it comes to publishing the best compilations of written music possible.

Having spent a major portion of my professional life accompanying vocalists, I was very excited about the prospect of working on a book primarily comprised of American standards. I am familiar with a multitude of wonderful songs that make up The Great American Songbook and was thrilled to be able to have as much input as I did in selecting the songs included here.

You will find songs that are familiar as well as lesser known gems that will make your musical life profoundly richer. Get ready to discover many beautiful melodies and lyrics. This is a collection that will be treasured for many years, I feel certain. I don't believe I am overstating the impact that this volume will have when I say that the instrumentalists and vocalists who work with these songs will raise the level of music in general.

This volume contains many of the greatest standards and jazz compositions ever written. A significant number have been recorded or performed only infrequently, in part because it has been very difficult to find accurate printed versions of them before now.

I urged Chuck to include verses whenever possible and it didn't take a lot to coax him into agreeing that they would be a valuable addition. In some cases the verses are not up to the quality of the song itself, but you will find forgotten verses (even to familiar songs) that will turn your head around. I feel that any vocalists who use this book should at least have the option of including the verses to songs they might want to perform.

Instrumentalists include the verses less often, but I'm sure some instrumentalists would want to include some of these. I presented the songs so the verses could easily be performed or not. All verses are clearly marked. Almost without exception they come before the song itself and set up the song. If you do not wish to include the verse, simple begin at letter A of any song (including the pickup notes.) Written instructions make it easy to perform the songs with solos and additional lyrics without including the verses. But please give yourself a treat and at least check them out.

You will notice something new in the inclusion of smaller size notes in some tunes. These are either harmony notes or accompanying figures. I thought it would be easier to distinguish them from the main melody notes if they were smaller. They can be disregarded without endangering the song, if you wish.

We listened to as many recordings of each song as was practical—often 15 or 20 versions of a frequently recorded song, attempting to distill out what are the chords most used by jazz vocalists and instrumentalists. These are the main changes. The alternate chords (in parenthesis) are chords less frequently used (but still good) or, in some cases, chords closer to the original sheet music. It was often very difficult to decide what chords to include here. " 'Round Midnight" comes to mind as a composition that had a very large number of harmonic choices. So the alternate changes are not exhaustive and please feel free to add your own reharmonizations as you see fit.

I want to thank some of the vocalists who have let me accompany their vocal flights. I have had the great pleasure of working with one of the world's great ballad singers, Bobbe Norris, since the late 1970s. Her warm and unique voice and her deep love of great songs are a constant inspiration to me. Some other singers I owe enormous debts to include Cleo Laine, Mark Murphy and Nancy King. They have led me on many a merry musical chase.

Along with Chuck I wish to thank Ernie Mansfield, Ann Krinitsky, Chuck Gee and Mark Levine for their great work in putting this book together. Some of the people who have introduced me to these songs include John Rogers, Jerry Dean, Bob Parlocha, Brailey Brown, David Friesen, Ernie Hood, Gene Esposito and George Moffatt. Thanks for the gift!

I can't wait to see what projects Sher Music Co. comes up with in the future. Just let me catch my breath, OK Chuck? Thanks for everything.

Larry Dunlap

GENERAL RULES FOR USING THIS BOOK

FORM

1. Key signatures will be found at the top of each page, as a rule. Any change of key will be noted not only where it occurs but also at the start of the next line. The key signature holds even if there is a change of clef, and is not restated. A change of key to C Major will appear as a clef followed by the naturals needed to cancel the previous key signature.
2. The coda sign is to be taken only when ending the tune unless otherwise stated. Some tunes have dual codas (Coda 1, Coda 2) to make it possible to fit a complex tune on two pages.
3. All repeats are observed during a 'D.C. al Coda' or 'D.S. al Coda' except in the following cases:
   a) when a Coda sign appears in a repeated section; the Coda is taken before repeating (unless marked 'on repeat'.)
   b) when an instruction to the contrary appears (e.g., 'D.S. al 2nd ending al Coda'.)
4. A Coda sign just within repeats is taken before repeating. A Coda sign just outside of repeats is taken after repeating.
5. When no solo form is specified, the whole tune is used for solos (except any Coda.)
6. 'Til Cue 'On Cue signifies dual endings for a section that repeats indefinately. The 'til cue' ending is played until cue, at which point the 'on cue' ending is played instead.
7. A section marked '4xs' is played four times.
8. A section marked 'ENDING' is played to end a tune; it directly follows the last bar of the head.

CHORDS

9. Chords fall on the beats over which they are placed.
10. Chords carry over to the next bar when no other chords or rests appear.
11. Chords in parentheses are optional except in the following cases:
    a) turn-arounds b) chords continued from the line before c) verbal comment explaining their use (e.g., for solos, for bass but not piano, only at certain times, etc.)
12. Optional chords in parentheses last as long as the chord they are written over or until the closing parenthesis is encountered, whichever is longer.
13. Written out piano or guitar voicings are meant to be played as written. Chord symbols appearing with such voicings often will not describe the complete voicing; they are meant to aid sight-reading and are often used for solos.
14. Multiple voices playing different rhythms are separated by having their stems lie in opposite directions whenever possible.

TERMS

15. An 'altered' dominant chord is one in which neither the fifth nor the ninth appears unaltered. Thus it contains b5 and/or #5, and b9 and/or #9.
16. 'Freely' signifies the absense of a steady tempo.
17. During a 'break. . . . . ' piano, bass and drums all observe the same rests. The last beat played is notated as ♪ or x to the left of the word 'break.'
18. A 'sample bass line', 'sample solo', or 'sample fill' are transcribed lines given as a point of reference.

TRANSPOSITIONS

19. Bass lines are always written to be read by a bass player, i.e. one octave higher than they sound.
20. Tenor sax and guitar lines are often written an octave higher than they sound and flute lines an octave lower to put them in a more readable range. There will be a verbal note to this effect in every case.
21. All horn and harmony parts are written in concert key (not transposed.)

ABBREVIATIONS

15ma. . . . . two octaves higher	elec. pn. . . . . electric piano	sop. . . . . soprano saxophone
15 ma b. . . . . . . two octaves lower	fl. . . . . flute	stac. . . . . staccato
8va . . . . one octave higher	gliss. . . . . glissando	susp. . . . . suspended
8va b . . . . one octave lower	gtr. . . . . guitar	synth. . . . . synthesizer
accel. . . . . accelerando	indef. . . . . indefinite (till cue)	ten. . . . . tenor saxophone
alt. . . . . altered	L.H. . . . . piano left hand	trb. . . . . trombone
bari. . . . . baritone saxophone	Med. . . . . Medium tempo	trbs. . . . . trombones
bkgr. . . . . background	N.C. . . . . No chord	trp. . . . . trumpet
bs. . . . . bass	Orig. . . . . Original	tpts. . . . . trumpets
cresc. . . . . crescendo	perc. . . . . percussion	unis. . . . . unison
decres. . . . . decrescendo	pn. . . . . piano	V.S. . . . . Volti Subito (quick page turn)
dr. . . . . drums	rall. . . . . rallentando	w/ . . . . with
elec. bs. . . . . electric bass	R.H. . . . . piano right hand	x . . . . time
	rit. . . . . ritard	x's . . . . times

ORNAMENTS AND SYMBOLS

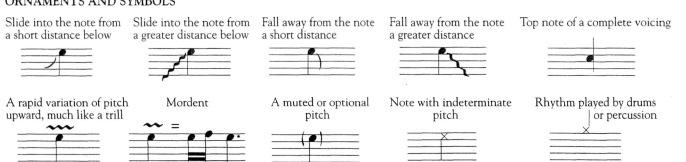

Slide into the note from a short distance below	Slide into the note from a greater distance below	Fall away from the note a short distance	Fall away from the note a greater distance	Top note of a complete voicing

A rapid variation of pitch upward, much like a trill	Mordent	A muted or optional pitch	Note with indeterminate pitch	Rhythm played by drums or percussion

CHORD SYMBOLS

The chord symbols in this book follow (with some exceptions) the system outlined in "Standard Chord Symbol Notation" by Carl Brandt and Clinton Roemer. It is hoped you will find them clear, complete and unambiguous.

Below are two groups of chord spellings.

1) The full range of chords normally encountered, given a C root, and

2) Some more unusual chords. (Note: some groups of notes below could be given different names, depending on context. See previous page for a definition of 'altered' chords.)

After You

(from "The Gay Divorcee")

Cole Porter

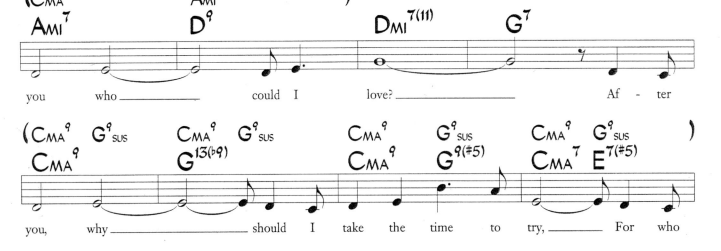

Solo on ABC
After solos, D.S. al fine

Again

Music by Lionel Newman
Lyric by Dorcas Cochran

Photo by Paul J. Hoeffler, Toronto

CARMEN McRAE

5

Agua De Beber
(Water To Drink)

Music by Antonio Carlos Jobim
English lyric by Norman Gimbel
Portuguese Lyric by Vinicius de Moraes

6

Additional English lyric:

The rain can fall on distant deserts.
The rain can fall upon the sea.
The rain can fall upon the flower.
Since the rain has to fall, let it fall on me.

Água de Beber (Portuguese lyric)

Eu quis amar mas tive medo.
E quis salvar meu coração.
Mas o amor sabe um segredo.
O medo pode matar o seu coração.

Água de beber, Água de beber camará.
Água de beber, Água de beber camará.

Eu nunca fiz coisa tão certa.
Entrei pra escola do perdão.
A minha casa vive aberta.
Abri todas as portas do coração.

Água de beber, Água de beber camará.
Água de beber, Água de beber camará.

Ain't No Sunshine

On the original Bill Withers version, the first ending is omitted (no repeat, no solo, very short).

Alice In Wonderland
(from "Alice In Wonderland")

Music by Sammy Fain
Lyric by Bob Hilliard
(As performed by Bill Evans.
Lyric as performed by Tom Lellis)

* Bill Evans plays all of this one octave higher, except the first 12 bars of letter B and the ad lib ending.

Alt text lyrics:

Al - ice In Won - der - land, Where is the path to Won - der - land? O - ver the hill or here or there? I won - der where. (fine)

(Take Coda for Bill Evans' ending)

Solo on ABC
After solos,
D.C. al Coda
(Vocal, D.C. al fine)

(Ad lib to end)
(loco)
(sample)
(Freely)

* Alternate chords for the last 4 bars of letter B:

All About Ronnie

Joe Green

All a-bout Ron - nie, There's so much to tell, _____ All a-bout

Ron - nie, I know {her}{him} so well. _____ {Her}{His}

mag - i - cal fin - gers, _____ their sense of em - brace, _____ {Her}{His}

per - fume{that lin - gers, _____ car - ess - ing your face. _____ All a - bout
whis - per}

Ron - nie, best told in a toast, _____ Let me pro -

pose it. {I'm her}{She's my} fav - 'rite host. _____ We'll

drink from dry glass - es, There's no need for wine. The cham-pagne is Ron - nie, _____

_____ And Ron - nie is mine.

Photo by Paul J. Hoewffler, Toronto

GLORIA LYNN

All My Tomorrows

Music by James Van Heusen
Lyric by Sammy Cahn

14

to. And all the dreams I dream, beg, or bor-row, on some bright to -

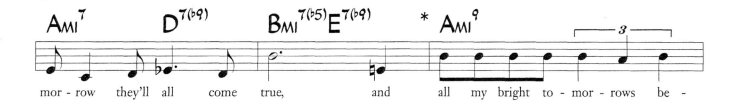

mor-row they'll all come true, and all my bright to-mor-rows be -

long to you.

* Optional ending

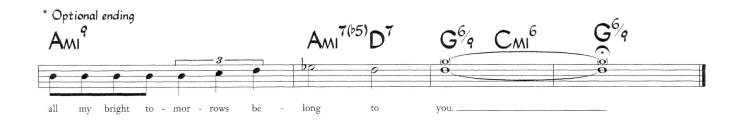

all my bright to-mor-rows be - long to you.

All Of You (Standard Version)

(from "Silk Stockings")

Cole Porter

* Alternate chords (Miles' version) sometimes do not fit the original melody.

Solo on AB
After solos, D.S. al fine

All Of You
(Bill Evans' Version)

Cole Porter
(As played by Bill Evans)

Note: Bill Evans does not play the original melody. The original melody has been altered here to better fit his changes.

BILL EVANS

All The Way
(from "The Joker Is Wild")

Music by James Van Heusen
Lyric by Sammy Cahn

When some-bod-y loves you, it's no good un-less {he}{she} loves you all the way.

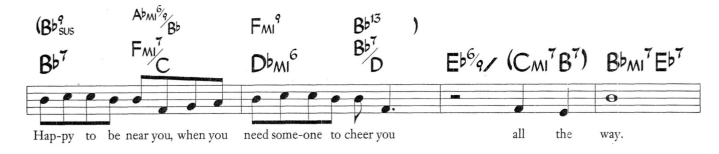

Hap-py to be near you, when you need some-one to cheer you all the way.

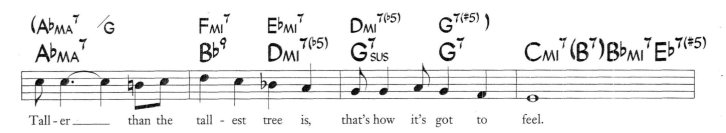

Tall-er ___ than the tall-est tree is, that's how it's got to feel.

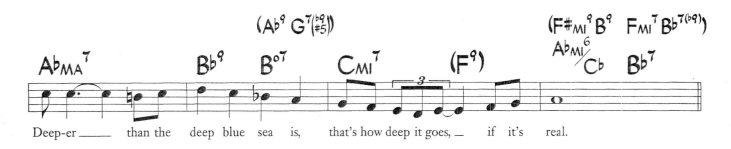

Deep-er ___ than the deep blue sea is, that's how deep it goes, ___ if it's real.

When some-bod-y needs you, it's no good un-less {he}{she} needs you, all the way.

Thru the good or lean years and for all the in be-tween years, come what may.

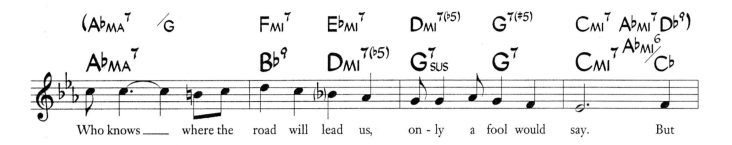

Who knows ___ where the road will lead us, on-ly a fool would say. But

if you let me love you, it's for sure I'm gon-na love you all the way,

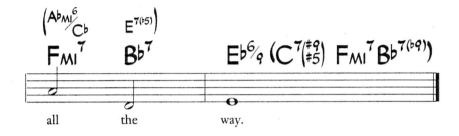

all the way.

All Through The Night
(from "Anything Goes")

Cole Porter

Medium

(Verse) F | FMI | F | FMI | F | FMI | F | FMI | F | FMI

The day __ is my en-e-my, __ The night __ is my friend, For I'm al-ways

F | FMI | F | FMI | F | FMI | F | FMI | F | FMI

so a-lone __ Till the day draws __ to an end, But when the sun goes down

F | FMI | Eb9sus Eb9 | AbMA7/Eb Ab6/Eb | Eb9sus Eb9 | AbMA7/Eb Ab6/Eb

And the moon comes through, To the mo-no-tone of the eve-ning's drone I'm

BbMI7 | FMI6 | GMI7(b5) C7 | FMA7 | GMI7 C7

all a-lone __ with you. __

(Medium)

𝄋 **A** FMA7 (DMI7 DbMI7 | CMI7 F7) | |
EMI7(b5) A7(b9) | DMI7 (Db7) CMI7 F7(b9) | BbMA7

All __ through the night __ I de-light __

BbMI7 Eb7(b9) | AbMA7 | (AbMI7 Db7) | AMI7(b5) D7(b9) | GMI7(b5)

__ in your love. All __ through the night __

C7(b9) | F6 | D7(b9) GMI7 | C7(b9)

__ you're so close to me. __

B FMA7 (DMI7 DbMI7 | CMI7 F7) | EMI7(b5) A7(b9) | DMI7(Db7) CMI7 F7(b9) | BbMA7 | BbMI7 Eb7(b9)

All __ through the night __ from a height __ far a-

Solo on ABCD
After solos, D.S. al fine

Jazz performers often alter the melody to

F^{MA7} E$^{MI7(b5)}$ A$^{7(b9)}$ D^{MI7} C^{MI7} F$^{7(b9)}$ B^b^{MA7}

or

F^{MA7} E$^{MI7(b5)}$ A$^{7(b9)}$ D^{MI7} C^{MI7} F$^{7(b9)}$ B^b^{MA7}

(etc.)

These chords are less structured than the original changes.
The melody fits this chart's chords with some liberty.

Alone Together

(from "Flying Colors")

Music by Arthur Schwartz
Lyric by Howard Dietz

Ballad or Medium

A - lone to - geth - er, Be-yond the crowd,

A - bove the world, We're not too proud to

cling to - geth - er. We're strong as long as we're to -

geth - er. A - lone to - geth - er,

The blind - ing rain, The star - less night,

Were not in vain; For we're to - geth - er, And

what is there to fear to - geth - er? Our

Am I Blue?

(from "On With The Show")

Music by Harry Akst
Lyric by Grant Clarke

BENNY GOODMAN

And The Angels Sing

Music by Ziggy Elman
Lyric by Johnny Mercer

Ballad or Medium

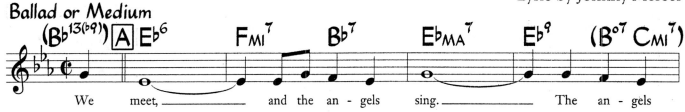

We meet, _____ and the an-gels sing. _____ The an-gels

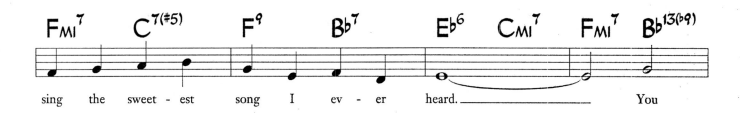

sing the sweet-est song I ev - er heard. _____ You

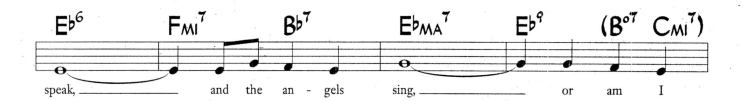

speak, _____ and the an-gels sing, _____ or am I

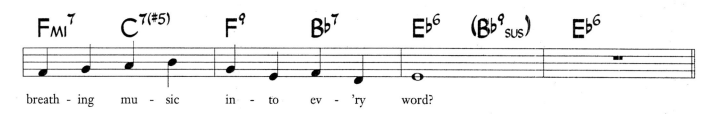

breath - ing mu - sic in - to ev - 'ry word?

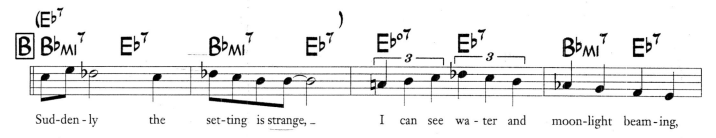

Sud-den-ly the set-ting is strange, _ I can see wa-ter and moon-light beam-ing,

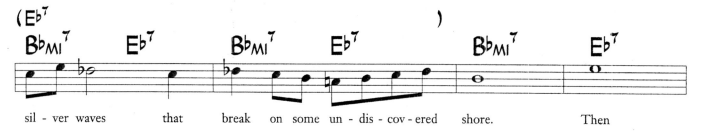

sil - ver waves that break on some un - dis - cov - ered shore. Then

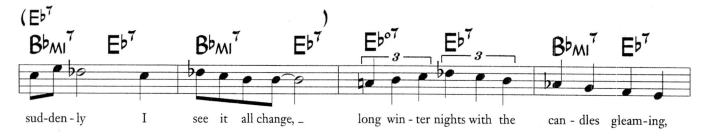

sud-den-ly I see it all change, _ long win-ter nights with the can - dles gleam-ing,

thru it all your face that I a - dore. _____ You

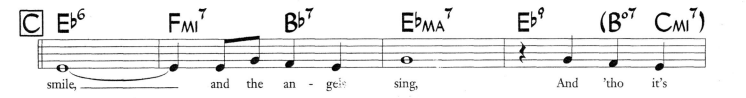

smile, _____ and the an - gels sing, And 'tho it's

just a gen - tle mur - mur at the start, _____ We

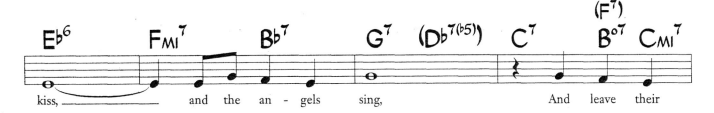

kiss, _____ and the an - gels sing, And leave their

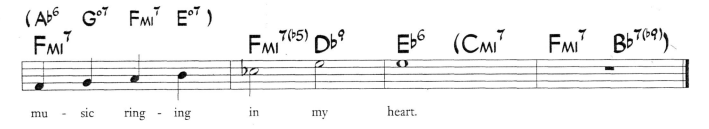

mu - sic ring - ing in my heart.

Anything Goes
(from "Anything Goes")

Cole Porter

30

As Time Goes By

(from "Casablanca")

Herman Hupfeld

This day and age we're liv-ing in gives cause for ap-pre-hen-sion, With speed and new in-ven-tion, and things like third di-men-sion, Yet, we grow a tri-fle wear-y, with Mis-ter Ein-stein's the-'ry, So we must get down to earth, at times re-lax, re-lieve the ten-sion. No mat-ter what the pro-gress, or what may yet be proved, The sim-ple facts of life are such they can-not be re-moved.

You must re-mem-ber this, a kiss is still a kiss, A sigh is just a sigh; The fun-da-men-tal things ap-ply, As time goes by.

As We Speak

David Sanborn
Michael Sembello

Pop/Samba Ballad, 2 Feel

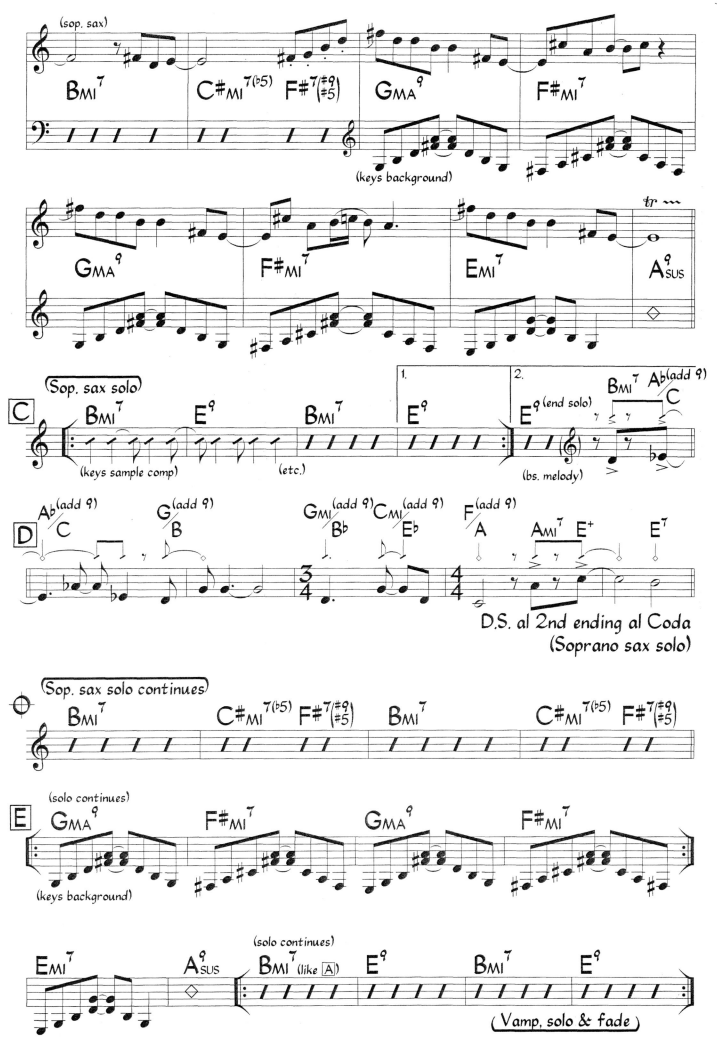

As We Speak (Bass)

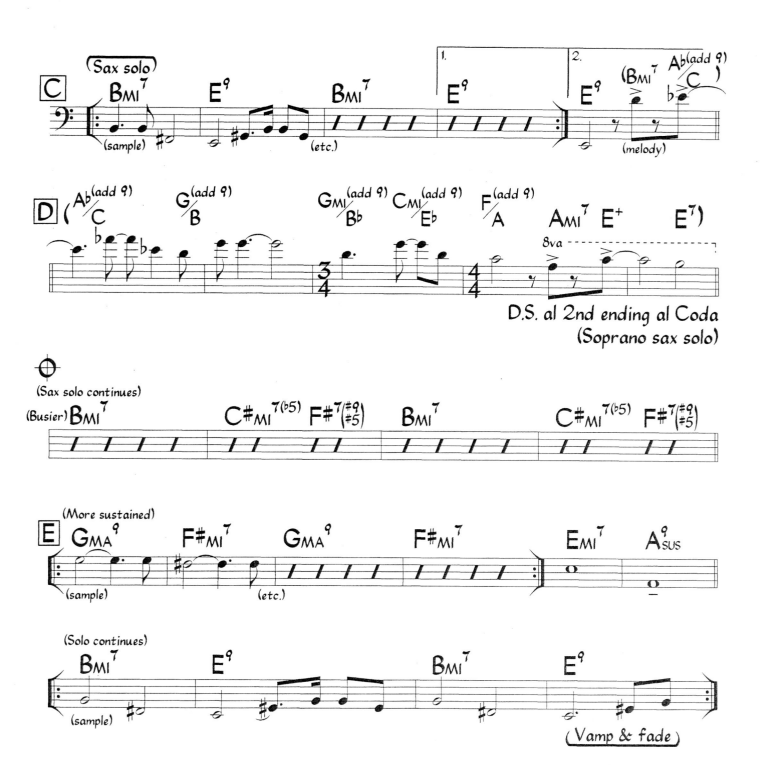

At Last
(from "Orchestra Wives")

Music by Harry Warren
Lyric by Mack Gordon

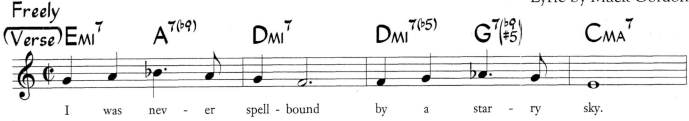

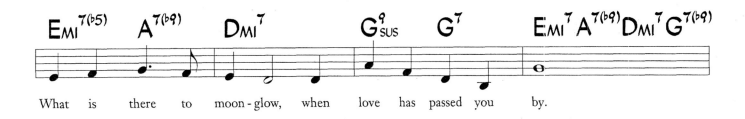

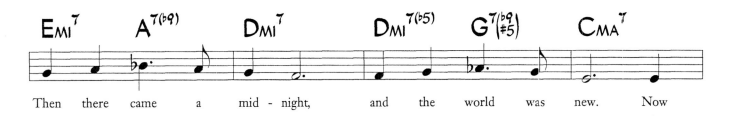

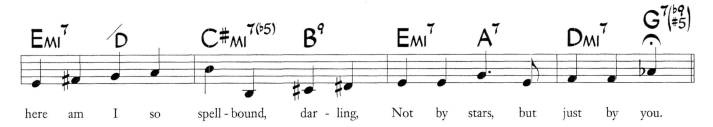

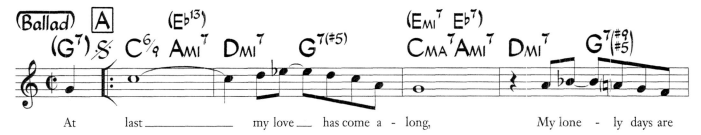

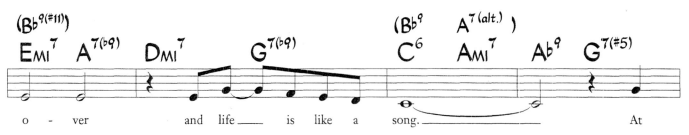

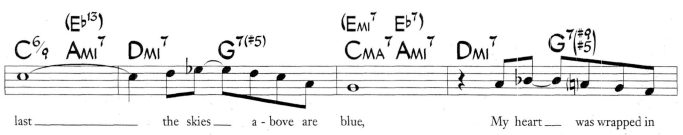

Solo on ABC
After solos, D.S. al fine

At Long Last Love
(from "You'll Never Know")

Cole Porter

Medium, Ala Rumba

(Verse)

I'm _____ so in love, _____ And though it gives me _____ joy in-

tense, _____ I can't de-ciph-er, _____ If I'm a lif-er, _____ Or if it's

just a _____ first of-fense. I'm _____ so in

love, _____ I've no sense of val-ues _____ left at all. _____ Is this a

play-time _____ af-faire of May-time, _____ Or is it a wind-fall? _____

(Medium or Ballad) A

Is it an earth-quake _____ or sim-ply a shock? _____ Is it the

good tur-tle soup or mere-ly the mock? _____ Is it a

cock-tail, _____ this feel-ing of joy, _____ Or is what I

Solo on AB
After solos, D.S. al fine

Autumn Nocturne

Music by Josef Myrow
Lyric by Kim Gannon

shad-ows bright Oc - to - ber's gold - en charms. The flam-ing moon re -

minds me of____ The night of love____ that____ we once knew._____ Each ti - ny

star is but a pray'r that when it's fall a - gain love will call a - gain

and you'll be be - side me to make my au - tumn dreams come true._____

true._____

— Solo on ABC
   After solos,
D.C. al last x ending

Original ending (each time)

true._____

D.C. for solos

Letter A, bars 8 and 15, and letter C, bar 6, are originally written

Bags' Groove

Milt Jackson

(melody)

(optional counter-melody)

(sample bass, optional tacet till letter B, 1st x only)

(lower notes are optional harmony)

B

(lower notes optional)

(optional counter-melody)
(bass etc.)

* The turns in the melody of the head are optional.

44

The Interlude is optional.

Baltimore Oriole
(from "To Have And Have Not")

Music by Hoagy Carmichael
Lyric by Paul Francis Webster

Medium Ballad*

Bal - ti-more O - ri - ole _____ took a look at the mer - cu - ry, for - ty be - low.

No life for a la - dy _____ to be drag - gin' her feath - ers a - round in the snow.

(Boy) Leav - ing me blue. _____
(Girl) Leav - ing her mate, _____

_____ off she flew
_____ she flew straight } to the Tan - gi - pa - ho _____ where a two - tim - in'

black - bird _____ met the di - vine _____ Miss O! I'd like to ruf -

- fle his plu - mage! Bal - ti-more O - ri - ole _____ messed a - roun' with that

big mouth 'til he singed her wing. For - giv - in' is eas - y, _____

46

it's a wom-an-like, now-and-then-could-hap-pen thing.

Send her back home, _____ home ain't home with-out her war-bl-ing; _____

Make a lone-ly man hap-py. _____ Bal-ti-more O-ri-

ole _____ come down _____ from that bough, _____

fly back _____ to me now.

Last four bars, alternate:

bough. Fly to your dad-dy now.

* Mark Murphy performs this Up Tempo. (One measure here equals two measures in Mark's version.)

A Beautiful Friendship

Music by Donald Kahn
Lyric by Stanley Styne

The rhythm of the melody is freely interpreted. It was originally written as follows:

BILLIE HOLIDAY

Begin The Beguine
(from "Jubilee")

Cole Porter

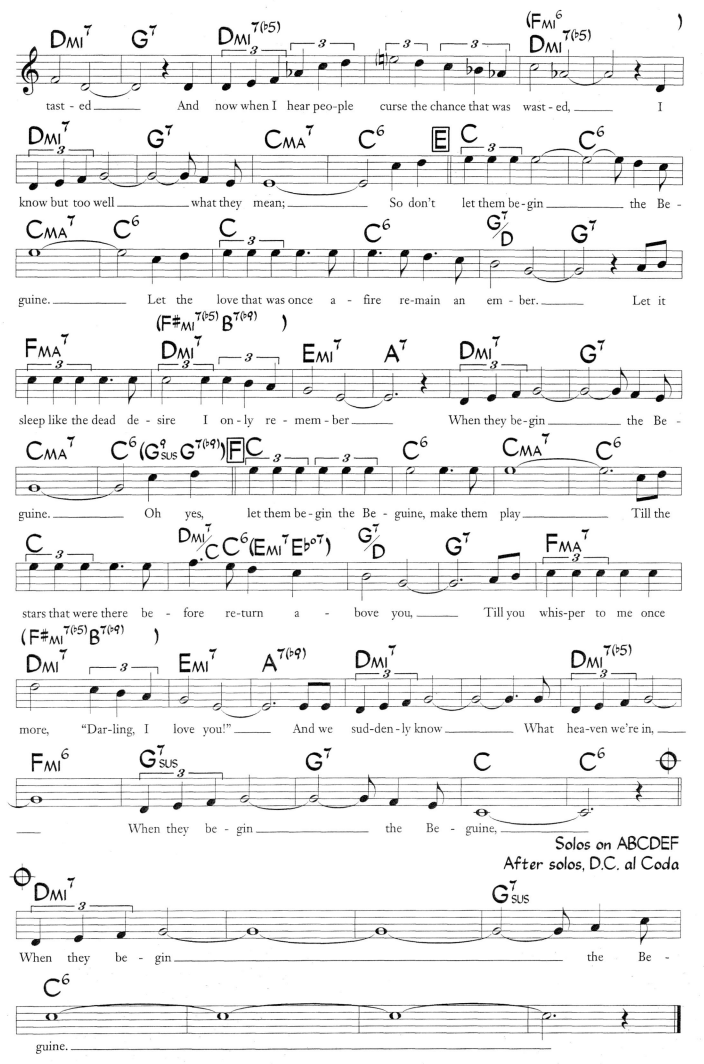

Solos on ABCDEF
After solos, D.C. al Coda

Bess, You Is My Woman
(from "Porgy And Bess")

George Gershwin
Ira Gershwin
Du Bose & Dorothy Heyward

This version is a composite of several instrumental versions.
The original vocal version is significantly different, so the lyric was not added here.

The Best Is Yet To Come

Music by Cy Coleman
Lyric by Carolyn Leigh

53

* Ignore chords in parentheses for solos.

(optional repeat for solo on ABCD)

Optional: vamp & fade on bars 3 & 4 from the end.

Bewitched
(from "Pal Joey")

Music by Richard Rodgers
Lyric by Lorenz Hart

Solo on ABC
After solos, D.S. al fine

* Letter A, bars 1-3 and 9-11 and letter C, bars 1-3 are often played or sung as follows (note the last note of the second bar):

(etc.)

Additional Lyric (as sung by Ella Fitzgerald)

<u>Verse</u>
After one whole quart of brandy, Like a daisy I'm awake.
With no Bromo Seltzer handy, I don't even shake.
Men are not a new sensation; I've done pretty well, I think.
But this half-pint imitation put me on the blink.

<u>Extra Refrains</u>

(I've) Seen* a lot — I mean a lot —
But now I'm like sweet seventeen a lot —
Bewitched, bothered and bewildered am I.
I'll sing to him, Each spring to him
And worship the trousers that cling to him —
Bewitched, bothered and bewildered am I.
When he talks, he is seeking
Words to get off his chest.
Horizontally speaking,
He's at his very best.
Vexed again, Perplexed again,
Thank God I can be oversexed again —
Bewitched, bothered and bewildered am I.

Wise at last, My eyes at last
Are cutting you down to your size at last —
Bewitched, bothered and bewildered no more.
Burned a lot, But learned a lot
And now you are broke, though you earned a lot —
Bewitched, bothered and bewildered no more.
Couldn't eat — Was dyspeptic,
Life was so hard to bear.
Now my heart's antiseptic,
Since you moved out of there.
Romance — finis; Your chance — finis;
Those ants that invaded my pants — finis —
Bewitched, bothered and bewildered no more.

* Ella sings "Sinned"   There is an original additional refrain that Ella does not sing.

Bidin' My Time
(from "Girl Crazy")

George Gershwin
Ira Gershwin

The form is sometimes performed AABC.

Blackberry Winter

Alec Wilder
Loonis McGlohon

Other alternate chords, at letter C only:

Blue And Sentimental

COLEMAN HAWKINS & MILES DAVIS

Blue Gardenia
(from "Blue Gardenia")

Bob Russell
Lester Lee

Blue Gar - den - ia, Thrown to a pass - ing breeze, But

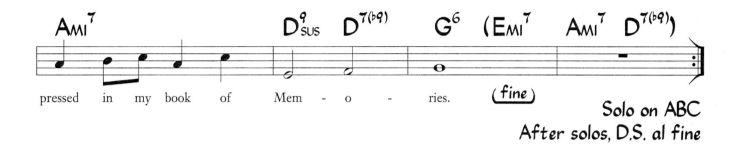

pressed in my book of Mem - o - ries. (fine)

Solo on ABC
After solos, D.S. al fine

Blue Room
(from "The Girl Friend")

Music by Richard Rodgers
Lyric by Lorenz Hart

Solo on ABC
After solos, D.S. al fine

Blues In The Night
(from "Blues In The Night")

Music by Harold Arlen
Lyric by Johnny Mercer

68

Bluesette

Music by Jean "Toots" Thielemans
Lyric by Norman Gimbel

Solo on C
After solos,
D.C. al Coda

Optional vamp & fade
on last 4 bars, using
alternate chords (in
parentheses)

In some versions, letters B and/or C are omitted.

Born To Be Blue

Mel Torme
Robert Wells

I guess I'm luck - i - er than some folks; _____ I've known the thrill of lov - ing

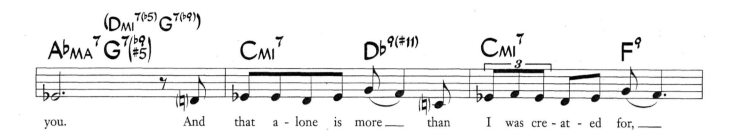

you. And that a - lone is more ____ than I was cre - at - ed for, ____

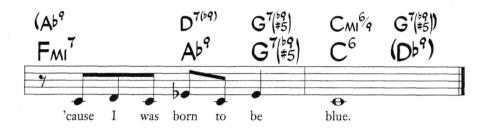

'cause I was born to be blue.

But Not For Me (Standard Version)

(from "Girl Crazy")

George Gershwin
Ira Gershwin

74

Solo on AB
After solos, D.S. al fine

75

But Not For Me
(Coltrane Version)

George Gershwin
Ira Gershwin
(As played by John Coltrane)

* This melody uses phrases from both the first and last choruses to make it as close to the original melody as was played.

76

Piano comps, disregarding bass notes, throughout.

Caught Up In The Rapture

Garry Glenn
Dianne Quander

(As performed by Anita Baker)

78

Charade

(from "Charade")

Music by Henry Mancini
Lyric by Johnny Mercer

Medium Waltz

When we played our cha - rade_____ We were like chil - dren pos - ing,_____ Play - ing at games, act - ing out names, Guess - ing the parts we played._____

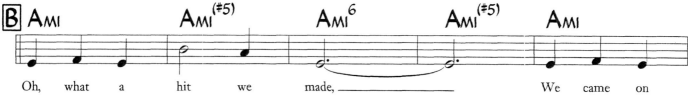

Oh, what a hit we made,_____ We came on

next to clos - ing;_____ Best on the bill, lov - ers un -

til love left the mas - que - rade._____

Fate_____ seemed to pull the strings, I turned

and you were gone._____ While_____ from the dark-ened

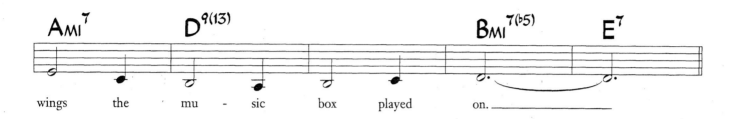
wings the mu - sic box played on._____

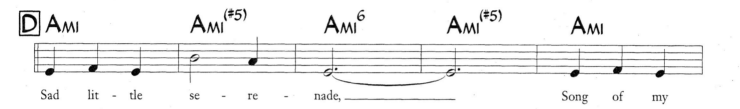
Sad lit-tle se - re - nade,_____ Song of my

heart's com - pos - ing;_____ I hear it still,

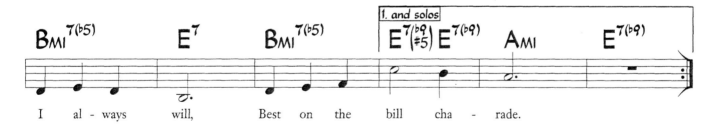
I al - ways will, Best on the bill cha - rade.

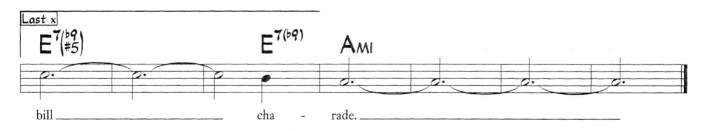
bill_____ cha - rade._____

The Christmas Waltz

Music by Jule Styne
Lyric by Sammy Cahn

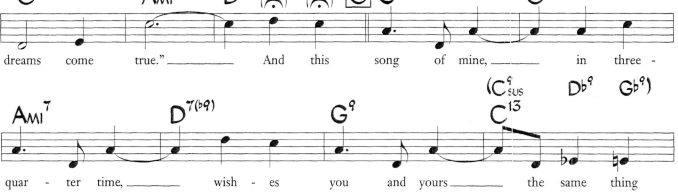

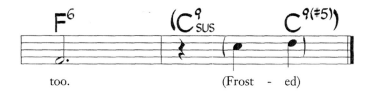

* In some versions the last 2 bars of letter B are expanded to 4 bars (with no fermatas).

ROY ELDRIDGE

Close Enough For Love

(from "Agatha")

Music by Johnny Mandel
Lyric by Paul Williams

Close To You

Music by Burt Bacharach
Lyric by Hal David

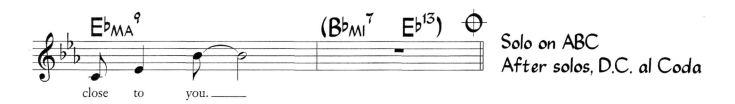

E♭MA⁹   (B♭MI⁷   E♭¹³)

close to you. _____

Solo on ABC
After solos, D.C. al Coda

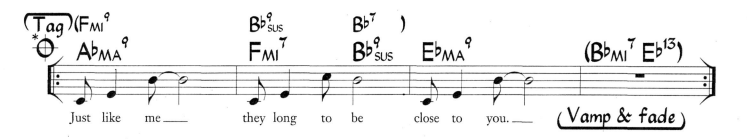

(Tag) (FMI⁹)   B♭⁹SUS   B♭⁷)
A♭MA⁹   FMI⁷   B♭⁹SUS   E♭MA⁹   (B♭MI⁷ E♭¹³)

Just like me _____ they long to be close to you. _____ (Vamp & fade)

* Optional Tag   (FMI⁷)
A♭MA⁹   E♭MA⁹

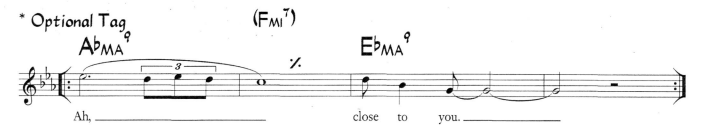

Ah, _____   close to you. _____

Letter A, bars 2 & 3 and 10 & 11, and letter C, bars 2 & 3, are often performed as follows:

(E♭¹³) [A] A♭MA⁹   G⁷SUS G⁷   GMI⁷   CMI⁷   (etc.)

Come Fly With Me

Music by
James Van Heusen
Lyric by Sammy Cahn

88

Solo on ABC
After solos, D.S. al fine

The Continental

Music by Con Conrad
Lyric by Herb Magidson

Cotton Tail
(a.k.a. Cottontail)

Duke Ellington

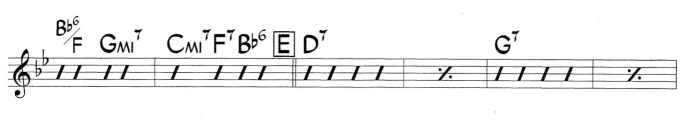

D.C. for more solos (AABC)
After solos, D.C. al Coda

* Kenny Clarke plays letter B, the bridge, like this:

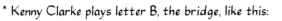

to letter C

Crazy He Calls Me

Music by Carl Sigman
Lyric by Bob Russell

Crazy Rhythm
(from "Here's How")

Music by Joseph Meyer
& Roger Wolfe Kahn
Lyric by Irving Caesar

I feel like the Em-per-or Ne-ro when Rome was a ve-ry hot
Ev-'ry Greek, each Turk and each La-tin, the Russ-ians and Pruss-ians as

town. Fath-er Knick-er-bock-er, for-give___ me, I
well, When they seek the lure of Man-hat-tan, are

play while your ci-ty burns down. Through all it's night life I
sure to come un-der your spell. Their na-tive folk songs they

fid-dle a-way.___ It's not the right life, but think of the pay.___
soon throw a-way.___ Those Har-lem smoke songs they soon learn to play.___

Some day I will bid it good-bye, __ I'll put my fid-dle a-way __ and I'll say:
Can't you fall for Car-ne-gie Hall; __ Oh, Dan-ny, call it a day __ and we'll say:

Cra-zy Rhy-thm, here's the door-way, I'll go my way,

you'll go your___ way, Cra-zy Rhy-thm, from now on___ we're

through. Here is where we have a show-down,

Bars 1-4 & 9-12 of letter A are sometimes played with these chords:

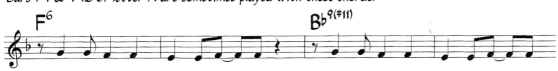

Cute

Neal Hefti

Repeat BC for solos
After solos, D.C. al 2nd ending al Coda

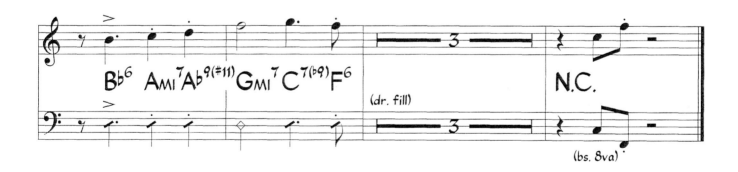

Dancing In The Dark

Music by Arthur Schwartz
Lyric by Howard Dietz

* Also played as a Samba.

(Optional Interlude)

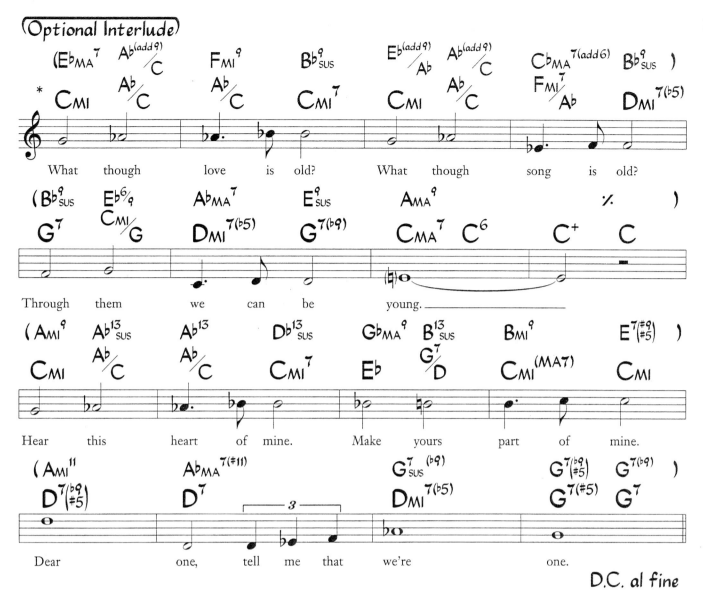

What though love is old? What though song is old?

Through them we can be young. _____

Hear this heart of mine. Make yours part of mine.

Dear one, tell me that we're one.

D.C. al fine

* Alternate chords for the Interlude are Fred Hersch's.
He plays the Interlude like this:

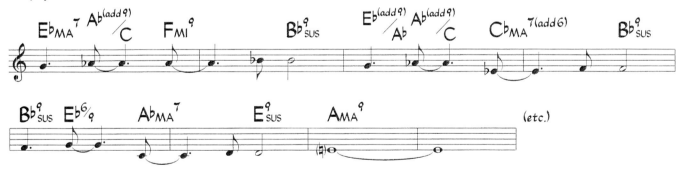

(etc.)

Most jazz performers (and others) do not include the Interlude.

Dancing On The Ceiling

(from "Evergreen")

Music by Richard Rodgers
Lyric by Lorenz Hart

* In Frank Sinatra's performance, the last four bars of the verse are omitted.

Solo on ABC.
After solos, D.S. al fine

Day In, Day Out

Music by Rube Bloom
Lyric by Johnny Mercer

104

Days Of Wine And Roses

(from "Days Of Wine And Roses")

Music by Henry Mancini
Lyric by Johnny Mercer

JOHNNY MERCER

Dedicated To You

Sammy Cahn
Saul Chaplin
H.H. Zaret

Solo on ABC
After solos, D.S. al fine

Deep Purple

Music by Peter De Rose
Lyric by Mitchell Parish

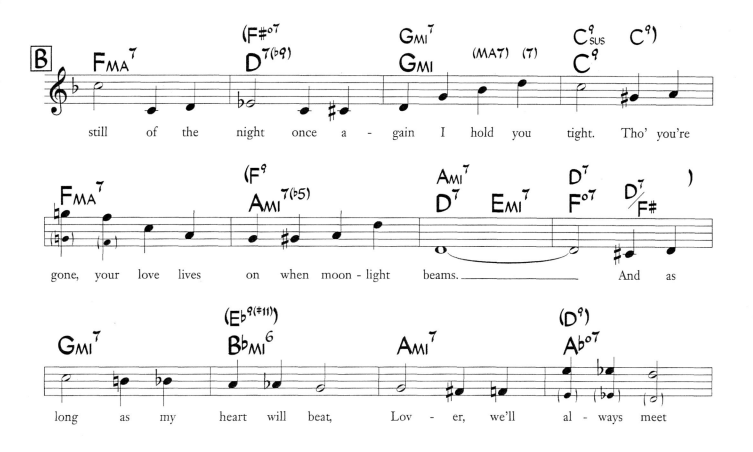

still of the night once a - gain I hold you tight. Tho' you're
gone, your love lives on when moon - light beams._____ And as

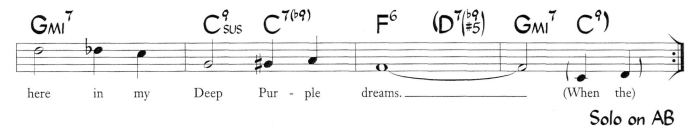

long as my heart will beat, Lov - er, we'll al - ways meet
here in my Deep Pur - ple dreams._____ (When the)

Originally the last note was C, except the final time when it was an F as written here.

Solo on AB
After solos, D.S. al fine

(Sittin' On) The Dock Of The Bay

Medium Slow 60's Folk/Rock

Otis Redding
Stephen Cropper

Don't Be Blue

Music by John Guerin
Lyric by Michael Franks

* Bass can walk over changes (with hits on the head) for the entire tune.

For additional solos,
Repeat letter C with 2nd ending
After solos, D.S. al Coda

out for your-self should be the rule. Give your

heart and your love to whom - ev - er you love, don't be a fool. Dar - ling,

why should you cling to some fad - ing thing that used to be? If

you can for - get, don't wor - ry 'bout me. (fine) Solo on AB
After solos, D.S. al fine

Doodlin'

Medium

Horace Silver

Piano plays letter A without added chords.

Doodlin' (Bass)

D.S. al Coda
(with repeat)

Photo © Lee Tanner/The Jazz Image

LAMBERT, HENDRICKS & ROSS

Doxy

Sonny Rollins

After solos, D.C. al Coda

Vamp & fade

The head is played twice at the beginning, one time after solos.

"Doxy" is played with many variations. Here is a version as played by Dexter Gordon.

Dream Dancing
(from "You'll Never Get Rich")

Cole Porter

* Also done as a Bossa Nova.

124

Solo on ABC.
After solos, D.S. al fine

Dreamsville

Music by Henry Mancini
Lyric by Jay Livingston & Ray Evans

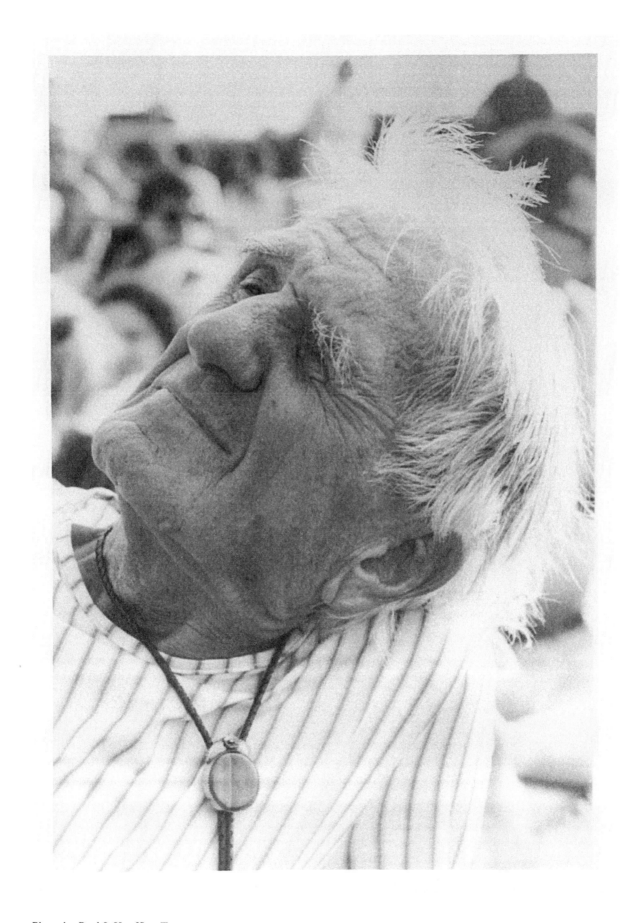

Photo by Paul J. Hoeffler, Toronto

GIL EVANS

Easy To Love
(from "Born To Dance")

Cole Porter

Originally written: (note bars 3 & 7)

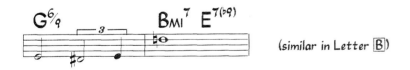

(similar in Letter B)

Embraceable You

(from "Girl Crazy")

George Gershwin
Ira Gershwin

Solo on AB.
After solos, D.S. al fine

Rhythm of melody is often altered to:
Letter A, bar 3, and similar measures throughout

Everything Must Change

Bernard Ighner

(Optional solos on AB)

Rain comes from the clouds, ___ sun lights up the sky, ___ and

hum - ming - birds do fly. ___ Rain comes from the clouds, ___

sun lights up the sky, ___ and mu - sic makes me cry. ___

Interlude from Quincy Jones' version. (Inserted before letter B, 2nd x)

(el. pn., plus 8va b.)

N.C. mp

(bs.)

Trombone solo

N.C.

(sample)

(Trombone solo etc.)

(Solo etc., busier feel)

(sample bs.)

mf

Ex - cept

Go to letter B
(take 2nd ending)

Falling In Love With Love

(from "The Boys Of Syracuse")

Music by Richard Rodgers
Lyric by Lorenz Hart

Medium or Bright
(see note at end)

134

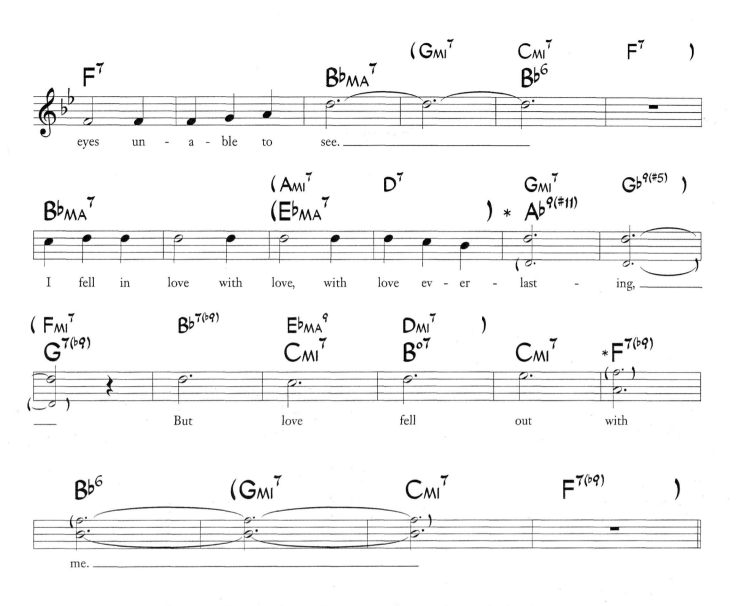

eyes un - a - ble to see. ____

I fell in love with love, with love ev - er - last - ing, ____

But love fell out with

me. ____

* Smaller notes (in parentheses) are the original notes. Larger notes are more frequently played or sung.

This piece is frequently played or sung in an Up Tempo 4 or 2:

(etc.)

Fascinating Rhythm
(from "Lady, Be Good")

George Gershwin
Ira Gershwin

136

Note: Last 3 bars are sometimes played:

Solo on ABCD
After solos, D.S. al fine

won't you stop pick - ing on me!   or   won't you stop pick - ing on me!

Originally in Eb, instrumentalists more often play this tune in F.

A Felicidade

Music by Antonio Carlos Jobim
Lyric by Vinicius de Moraes

Medium Samba (Ami⁹)

1. Tris - te - za não tem fim ___ Fe - li -
2. (Tris - te) - za não tem fim ___ Fe - li -

ci - da - de sim. ___
ci - da - de sim. ___

A fe - li - ci - da - de é co - mo_a go - ta De or - va -
A fe - li - ci - da - de é co - mo_a plu - ma Que_o - ven -

lho nu - ma pé - ta - la ___ de flor. ___
to vai ___ le - van - do pe - lo ar. ___

Bri - lha ___ tran - qüi - la ___ De - pois ___ de le - ve_os - ci - la E cai
Vo - a ___ tão le - ve Mas tem ___ a vi - da bre - ve Pre - ci -

com mo_u - ma lá - gri - ma ___ de a - mor.
sa que_ha - ja ven - to sem ___ pa - rar.

A fe - li - ci - da - de do po - bre pa - re - ce ___ A ___
A fe - li - ci - da - de ___ es - ta so - nhan - do ___ Nos

___ gran - de_i - lu - são ___ do car - na - val. ___ A gen -
___ o - lhos ___ da mi - nha na - mo - ra - da. ___ É co -

* In some versions letter A is repeated. (Form: AABCD)

A Foggy Day
(from "A Damsel In Distress")

George Gershwin
Ira Gershwin

140

Forest Flower

Charles Lloyd

142

From This Moment On
(from "Kiss Me Kate")

Cole Porter

Get Here

Brenda Russell

Get Out Of Town

(from "Leave It To Me")

Cole Porter

Just dis - ap-pear, __ I care __ for you much too much, __ And

when you are near, __ close to me, dear, __ We touch too much, __

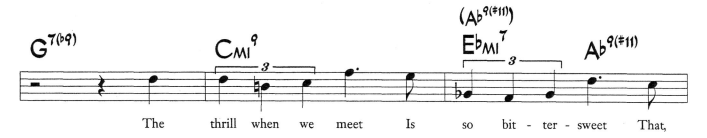

The thrill when we meet Is so bit - ter - sweet That,

dar - ling, it's get - ting me down. __ So on your mark, __ get

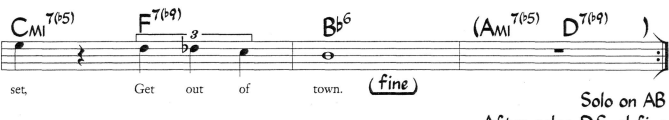

set, Get out of town. (fine)

Solo on AB
After solos, D.S. al fine

149

The Girl From Ipanema

(Garôta de Ipanema) Music by Antonio Carlos Jobim
Portuguese Lyric by Vinicius de Moraes
English lyric by Norman Gimbel

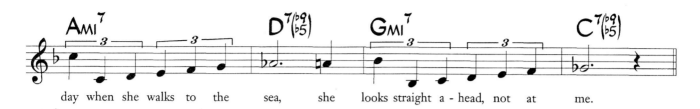

day when she walks to the sea, she looks straight a - head, not at me.

Tall and tan and young____ and love - ly, The Girl____ From I - pa - ne -

ma goes walk - ing, and when____ she pass - es I smile, ____ but she does - n't

see.

Solo on ABC
After solos, D.C. al Coda

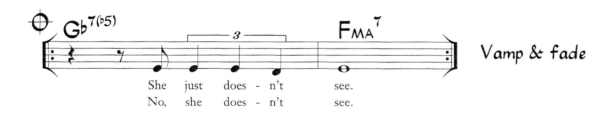

She just does - n't see.
No, she does - n't see.

Vamp & fade

Girl From Ipanema (Garota de Ipanema) Portuguese Lyric
(The melody rhythm with the Portuguese lyric is considerably different.)

Olha que coisa mais linda, Mais cheia de graça,
E ela menina Que vem e que passa,
Num doce balanço, caminho do mar.

Moça do corpo dourado, Do sol de Ipanema,
O seu balançado é mais que um poema,
É a coisa mais linda que eu já ve passar.

Ah!, porque estou tão sozinha.
Ah!, porque tudo é tão Triste.
Ah!, a beleza que existe.
A beleza que nào é só minha, Que também passa sozinha.

Ah!, se ela soubesse Que quando ela passa
O mundo sorrindo se enche de graça
E fica mais lindo Por causa do amor.

152

153

Good Bait

154

The Good Life

Music by Sacha Distel
Lyric by Jack Reardon
and Jean Broussolle

156

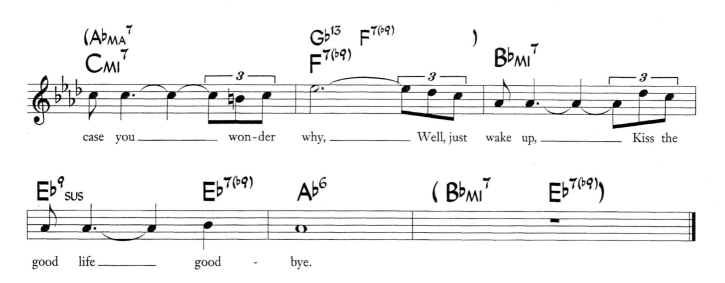

good life_____ good - bye.

The last line was originally: "Please remember I still love you, and in case you didn't know,
Well, just wake up, Kiss the good life hello."

Have You Met Miss Jones?

(from "I'd Rather Be Right")

Music by Richard Rodgers
Lyric by Lorenz Hart

158

He Was Too Good To Me
(from "Simple Simon")

Music by Richard Rodgers
Lyric by Lorenz Hart

smile, _____ that was his fun. _____

When I was mean to him He'd nev-er say, "Go 'way now."

I was a queen to him. Who's goin' to make me gay now?

It's on-ly nat-u-ral I'm blue,

He was too good to be true. (fine)

Solo on AB
After solos, D.S. al fine

The original melody varies considerably from this version.
This version is based on recordings by Chet Baker and Meredith D'Ambrosio.

160

Hello

Lionel Richie
*

* The melody is freely interpreted.

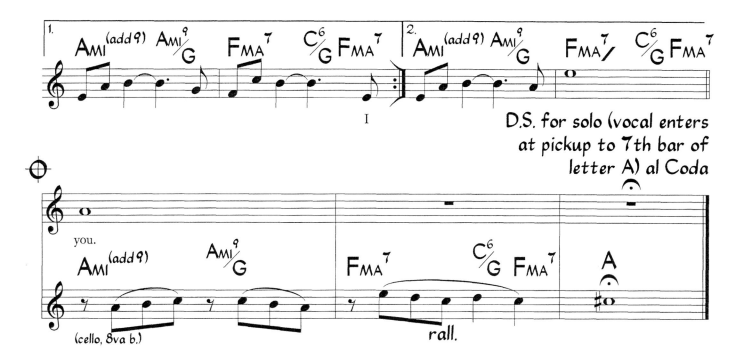

In the original version by Lionel Richie, the instrumental solo (D.S.) is only 6 bars long and the vocal that follows is:

Hello, is it me you're looking for?
'Cause I wonder where you are
And I wonder what you do,
Are you somewhere feeling lonely
Or is someone loving you?
Tell me how to win your heart,
For I haven't got a clue,
But let me start by saying "I love you."

Hey There

(from "The Pajama Game")

Richard Adler
Jerry Ross

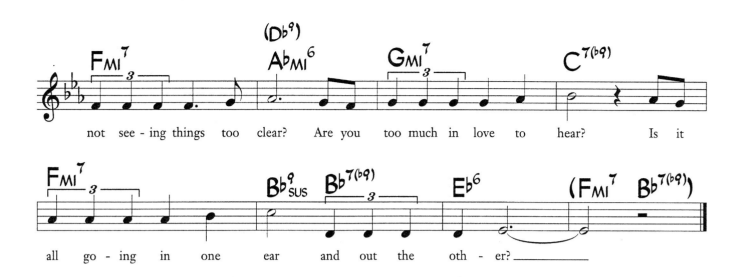

not see - ing things too clear? Are you too much in love to hear? Is it

all go - ing in one ear and out the oth - er?

Most of the alternate chords are from Hal Galper's great version.

Hot House

Up Tempo, Bebop

Tadd Dameron

Bars 1-4 of A and D are often played:

Based on the chords of "What Is This Thing Called Love?"

THELONIOUS MONK

A House Is Not A Home

Music by Burt Bacharach
Lyric by Hal David

When it ends_____ it ends in tears. Dar - ling, have a heart.___

Don't let one mis - take keep us a - part. I'm not

meant to live a - lone. Turn this house in - to a home. When I climb the stair____ and turn the

key, Oh, please be there still in love with me.

Bridge in chart (letter B) is as played by McCoy Tyner.
The original bridge is as follows:

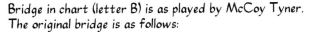

Now and then I call your name and sud - den - ly your face ap - pears.____

_____ But it's just____ a cra - zy game.____ When it ends it ends in tears.

How Do You Keep The Music Playing?

Music by Michel Legrand
Lyric by Alan and Marilyn Bergman

How Insensitive
(Insensatez)

Music by Antonio Carlos Jobim
Portuguese Lyric by Vinicius de Moraes
English lyric by Norman Gimbel

In your arms I know for once in my life I'm liv - ing.

C Had a good time___ ev - 'ry time I went out.___ Ro - mance was a thing___ I

kid - ded a - bout.___ How could I know a - bout love?_____ I did - n't know a - bout

you. *(fine)*

Solo on ABC
After solos, D.S. al fine

I Didn't Know What Time It Was

(from "Too Many Girls")

Music by Richard Rodgers
Lyric by Lorenz Hart

I Get A Kick Out Of You

(from "Anything Goes")

Cole Porter

190

* Upper notes are the original notes, lower notes are often used.

Solo on ABCD
After solos, D.S. al fine

Note

rhythm is usually played or sung as

I Got Rhythm

(from "Girl Crazy")

George Gershwin
Ira Gershwin

Letter A bars 5-6 and 13-14, and letter C, bars 5-6, can also use the following chords:

Jazz instrumentalists often use the "shorter" ending, making letter C 8 bars long.

I Gotta Right To Sing The Blues

(from "Earl Carroll's Vanities")

Music by Harold Arlen
Lyric by Ted Koehler

Solo on AB
After solos, D.S. al fine

I Guess I'll Have To Change My Plan

Music by Arthur Schwartz
Lyric by Howard Dietz

196

fore I knew where I was at_____ I found my-self up-on the shelf, and that was
boil-ing point is much too low_____ For me to try to be a fly Lo-tha-ri-

that. I tried to reach the moon but when I got there,
o! I think I'll crawl right back and in-to my shell,

All that I could get was the air. My feet are back up-on the
Dwell-ing in my per-son-al Hell. I'll have to change my plan a-

ground, I've lost the one girl I found. *fine* (I)
round,

Solo on ABC
After solos, D.S. al fine

I Had The Craziest Dream

(from "Springtime In The Rockies")

Music by Harry Warren
Lyric by Mack Gordon

long can a guy___ go on dream - ing?___ If there's a chance___ that you care___
gal___

___ Then, please say you do; (Ba - by)

Say it and make___ my craz - i - est dream___ come true.___ (fine) Solo on ABC
After solos, D.S. al fine

I Have The Feeling I've Been Here Before

Music by Roger Kellaway
Lyric by Alan & Marilyn Bergman

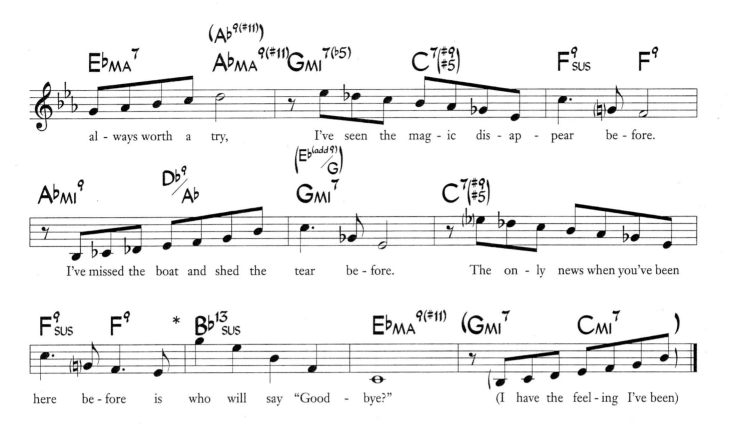

al - ways worth a try, I've seen the mag - ic dis - ap - pear be - fore.

I've missed the boat and shed the tear be - fore. The on - ly news when you've been

here be - fore is who will say "Good - bye?" (I have the feel - ing I've been)

* Also performed (Carmen McRae):

who will say "Good - bye?"

I Love Paris
(from "Can-Can")

Cole Porter

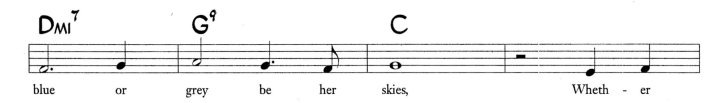

Ev - 'ry time I look down on this time - less town, wheth - er

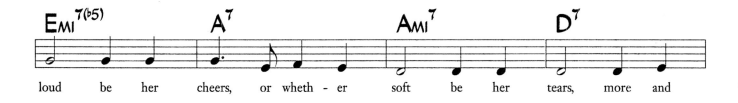

blue or grey be her skies, Wheth - er

loud be her cheers, or wheth - er soft be her tears, more and

more do I re - al - ize, (that) (optional)

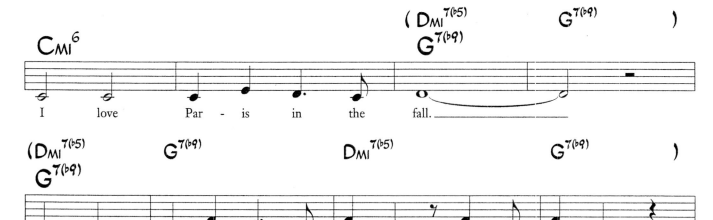

I love Par - is in the spring - time.

I love Par - is in the fall.

I love Par - is in the win - ter, when it driz - zles.

* Also done Up Tempo. (Sometimes Letter A is Latin and Letter B is Jazz Swing.)

202

Optional ending is from the original sheet music.
Some instrumental versions repeat letter A. (Form = AAB)

I Love You

(from "Mexican Hayride")

Cole Porter

204

Optional ending is from the original sheet music.

I Loves You Porgy
(from "Porgy And Bess")

George Gershwin
Ira Gershwin
Du Bose & Dorothy Heyward

205

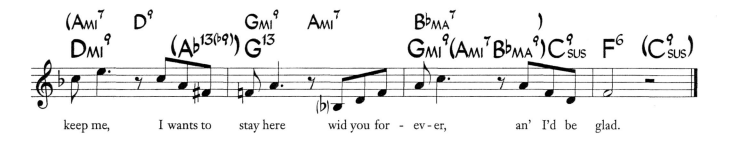

keep me,   I wants to   stay here   wid you for - ev-er,   an' I'd be glad.

This version is based on several different instrumental versions.
*The original version does not repeat letter A. The form is ABA, with the 1st ending omitted.
The original version has other sections not included in this chart.
The lyrics of letters A and C are sometimes reversed.

206

207

I May Be Wrong
(But I Think You're Wonderful)

Music by Henry Sullivan
Lyric by Harry Raskin

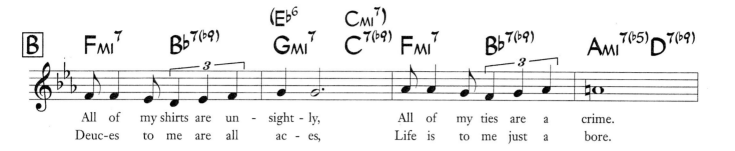

All of my shirts are un - sight - ly, All of my ties are a crime.
Deuc-es to me are all ac - es, Life is to me just a bore.

If, dear, in you I've picked right - ly, It's the ve - ry first time.
Fac - es are all op - en spac - es, You might be John Bar - ry - more.

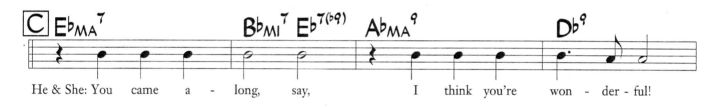

He & She: You came a - long, say, I think you're won - der - ful!

I think you're grand, but, I may be wrong.

(fine)
Solo on ABC
After solos, D.S. al fine

I Only Have Eyes For You

(from "Dames")

Music by Harry Warren
Lyric by Al Dubin

I Say A Little Prayer For You

Music by Burt Bacharach
Lyric by Hal David

I Want To Be Happy

(from "No, No, Nanette")

Music by Vincent Youmans
Lyric by Irving Caesar

Solo on ABC
After solos, D.S. al fine

Originally written:

(etc.)

I Was Doing All Right

(from "The Goldwyn Follies")

George Gershwin
Ira Gershwin

Freely (GMA⁷
(**Verse**) G

Used to lead a qui-et ex-ist-ence, Al-ways had my peace of mind.

Kept Old Man Trou-ble at a dis-tance; My days were sil-ver lined.

Right on top of the world I sat, But look at me now, ___ I don't know where I'm at. ___

Medium
A

I was do-ing all right, Noth-ing but rain-bows in my sky.

I was do-ing all right till you came by.

Had no cause to com-plain, Life was as sweet as ap-ple pie.

Solo on ABC
After solos, D.S. al fine

I Will Be Here For You

Richard Page
Steve George
John Lang
(As performed by Al Jarreau)

* On Al Jarreau's version there are no solos. (Form: ABC AB Coda)

I Will Be Here For You (Rhythm Section & Horns)

* On Al Jarreau's version there are no solos. (Form: ABC AB Coda)

I Will Wait For You

(from "The Umbrellas Of Cherbourg")

Music by Michel Legrand
Original French text
by Jacques Demy
English lyric by Norman Gimbel

I Wish I Knew

(from Billy Rose's "Diamond Horseshoe")

Music by Harry Warren
Lyric by Mack Gordon

223

224

Don't lead me on, If I'm a fool just say so.

Should I keep dream-ing on, or just for-get you?

What shall I do, I wish I knew. (fine)

Solo on ABCD
After solos, D.S. al fine

Bill Evans' changes (very slow Ballad)

Note: These chords do not always fit the melody.

I Wish I Were In Love Again

(from "Babes In Arms")

Music by Richard Rodgers
Lyric by Lorenz Hart

fly - ing plates, }
pair of heels, }
I wish I were in love a - gain!

No _____ more pain,
No _____ more care,
No _____ more strain,
No _____ de - spair,

Now _____ I'm sane, but _____
I'm _____ all there now, _____
I would rath - er be ga - ga! _____ The
But I'd rath - er be punch-drunk! _____ Be -

pulled out fur of cat and cur, The fine mis - mat - ing of a
lieve me, sir, I much pre - fer The clas - sic bat - tle of a

him and her, I've learned my les - son, but }
him and her, I don't like qui - et and }
I wish I were in

love a - gain! (fine) (The)

Solo on ABC
After solos, D.S. al fine

226

* Two bars before letter C, the break is optional (head only).

I'm A Fool To Want You

Frank Sinatra
Jack Wolfe
Joel Herron

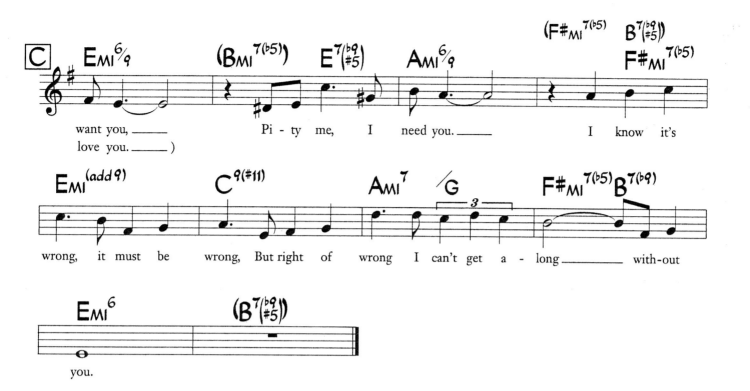

want you, _____
love you. _____)
Pi - ty me, I need you._____
I know it's

wrong, it must be wrong, But right of wrong I can't get a - long_____ with-out

you.

I'm Gonna Laugh You Right Out Of My Life

Music by Cy Coleman
Lyric by Joseph A. McCarthy

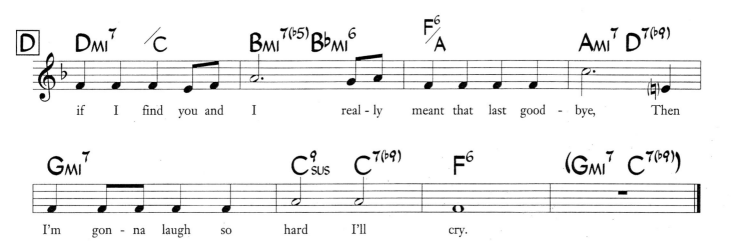

if I find you and I real-ly meant that last good-bye, Then

I'm gon-na laugh so hard I'll cry.

I've Got A Crush On You
(from "Strike Up The Band")

George Gershwin
Ira Gershwin

He: How glad the man-y mil-lions of An-na-belles and Lill-ians would be ⟧ to cap-ture
She: How glad a mil-lion lad-dies from mill-ion-aires to cad-dies would be ⟧

me! But you had such per-sist-ence, you broke down my re-sist-ance. I

fell, and it was swell. She: You're my big and brave and hand-some Ro-me-o.

How I won you I shall nev-er, nev-er know. He: It's not that you're at-trac-tive, But,

oh, my heart grew ac-tive when you came in-to view.

He: I've got a crush on you, Sweet-ie Pie.
She: I've got a crush on you, Sweet-ie Pie.

All the day and night-time hear me sigh. I nev-er had the least
All the day and night-time hear me sigh. This is-n't just a flir-

C¹³   GMI⁹   C¹³   CMI⁹   F⁹

no - tion _____ that I could fall with _____ so much e - mo - tion.
ta - tion. _____ We're prov-ing that there's _____ pre - des - ti - na - tion.

B   (DMI⁷)   B♭MA⁷   D♭°⁷   CMI⁷   F¹³⁽ᵇ⁹⁾   (DMI⁷) B♭MA⁷   D♭°⁷

Could you coo, _____ Could you care _____ for a cun - ning cot - tage
I could coo, _____ I could care _____ for that cun - ning cot - tage

CMI⁷   A♭⁹   (AMI⁷⁽ᵇ⁵⁾ D⁷⁽ᵇ⁹⁾ GMI⁷)   B♭MA⁷   GMI⁷   ⊕C¹³ / DMI⁷ GMI⁷

we could share? __ The world will par - don my mush, 'Cause I've got a
we could share? __ Your mush I nev - er shall shush, 'Cause I've got a

C⁹   F¹³   B♭⁶   (F⁷)

crush, my ba - by, on you. (fine) I've got a
crush, my ba - by, on you.

Solo on AB
After solos, D.S. al fine

⊕ Optional longer ending

C¹³ (A⁷⁽ᵇ⁹⁾) DMI⁷ GMI⁷   C⁹   F¹³   B♭⁶ (GMI⁷ C⁹ / F⁹ˢᵁˢ F⁷)

mush, 'Cause I've got a crush, my ba - by, on you. _____

* This song is most often performed as a ballad.
However, it was originally written as follows:

Bright, gaily   B♭MA⁷   B♭°⁷   CMI⁷   F⁷

I've got a crush on you, _____ Sweet - ie Pie. _____ (etc.)

I've Got You Under My Skin

(from "Born To Dance")

Cole Porter

Letter B, bars 1 through 6, are often played over an Eb pedal.

* Letter B is usually performed as follows:

235

If There Is Someone Lovelier Than You

Music by Arthur Schwartz
Lyric by Howard Dietz

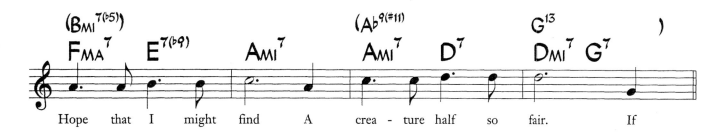

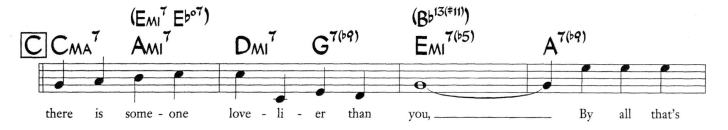

Solo on A B C
After solos, D.S. al fine

Red Garland's ending:

In The Days Of Our Love

(aka "Afterglow")

Music by Marian McPartland
Lyric by Peggy Lee

JON HENDRICKS & BOBBY MCFERRIN

In The Midnight Hour

Medium Motown Rock

Music by Steve Cropper
Lyric by Wilson Pickett

(horns)
(drums play thru)

(bs.)

(etc.)

I'm gon-na

wait til the mid-night hour, _____ that's when my love comes tum-bl-ing _____
wait til stars come out _____ and see the twin-kle in your eyes, _____

down. _____ I'm gon-na wait til the mid-night hour, _____ when there's
_____ I'm gon-na wait til the mid-night hour, _____ that's when my

no one else _____ a-round. _____ I'm gon-na take you, girl, and hold _____
love be-gins _____ to shine. _____ You're the on-ly girl I know _____

_____ you, and do all the things _____ I told _____ you in the mid-night hour. _____
that

Yes, I am, oh yes, I am. _____ I'm gon-na

real-ly loves _____ me so _____ in the mid-night hour, _____ oh yeah,

240

241

Indian Summer

Music by Victor Herbert
Lyric by Al Dubin

EDDIE SAFRANSKY

Isn't It A Pity?
(from "Pardon My English")

George Gershwin
Ira Gershwin

It Ain't Necessarily So
(from "Porgy And Bess")

George Gershwin
Ira Gershwin
Du Bose & Dorothy Heyward
(As played by Joe Henderson)

The Interlude was originally inserted between repeated A sections (with subsequent verses) (A, Interlude, A, Interlude, ABCG)
Many colloquial words have been normalized. ("That" for "Dat", "Heaven" for "Hebben", etc.)

It Had To Be You

Music by Isham Jones
Lyric by Gus Kahn

Why do I do just as you say, ___ why must I just give you your way? ___
Seems like dreams like I al-ways had ___ could be, should be mak-ing me glad.

Why do I sigh, ___ why don't I try ___ to for - get? It must have
Why am I blue? ___ It's up to you ___ to ex - plain. I'm think - ing

been that some-thing lov-ers call fate, ___ kept on say - ing I had to wait. ___
may - be, ba - by, I'll go a - way ___ some day, some way you'll come and say, ___

I saw them all, ___ just could - n't fall ___ 'til we met. ___
"It's you I need," ___ and you'll be plead - ing in vain. ___

It had to be you, ___ it had to be you. ___ I wan-dered a-round ___

___ and fin - al - ly found ___ the some-bod - y who ___ Could make me be true, ___

could make me be blue ___ And e - ven be glad, ___

just to be sad, ____ think-ing of you. ____ Some oth-ers I've seen ____

might nev-er be mean, ____ Might nev-er be cross ____

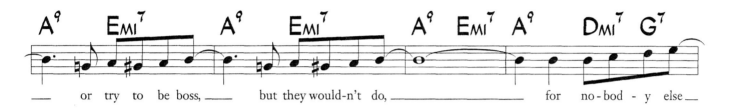

or try to be boss, ____ but they would-n't do, ____ for no-bod-y else ____

gave me a thrill, ____ with all your faults ____ I love you still. ____ It had to be you, ____

won-der-ful you, ____ had to be you. ____ *(fine)* (It had to be you, ____)

Solo on AB
After solos, D.S. al fine

It Never Entered My Mind

(from "Higher And Higher)

Music by Richard Rodgers
Lyric by Lorenz Hart

Solo on ABC
After solos, D.S. al fine

Originally written:

(etc.)

It Was A Very Good Year

Ervin Drake

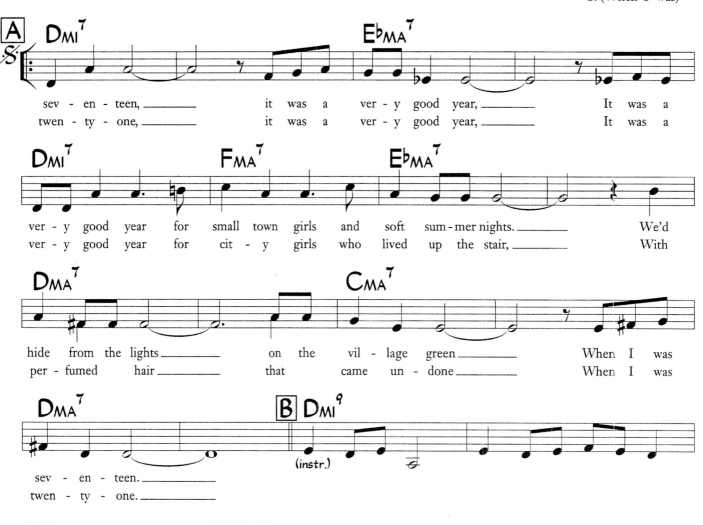

Additional Verses:

3. When I was thirty-five,
   it was a very good year,
   It was a very good year
   for blue-blooded girls of independent means.
   We'd ride in limousines
   their chauffeurs would drive
   When I was thirty-five.

4. But now the days are short,
   I'm in the autumn of the year
   And now I think of my life
   as vintage wine from fine old kegs.
   From the brim to the dregs
   it poured sweet and clear,
   It was a very good year.

JEAN "TOOTS" THIELEMANS

It's All Right With Me

(from "Can-Can")

Cole Porter

* Letter A, bars 11-12 and 27-28 and Letter C, bars 11-12 are written as they are most often performed.
The original melody was written:

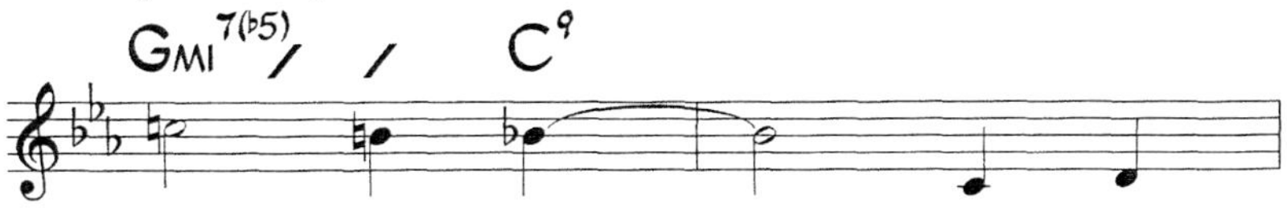

It's De-lovely
(from "Red, Hot And Blue")

Cole Porter

* Pronounced "de-lukes"

Solo on ABC
After solos, D.S. al fine

It's Magic
(from the film "Romance On The High Seas")

Music by Jule Styne
Lyric by Sammy Cahn

things be-gin when I am in your arms.

When we walk hand in hand the world be-comes a won-der-land, It's mag - ic.

How else can I ex-plain those rain-bows when there is no rain, It's mag - ic. Why do I

tell my - self these things that hap - pen are all real - ly true,

When in my heart I know the mag - ic is my love for you. (fine)

Solo on ABCD

After solos, D.S. al fine

It's You Or No One
(from "Romance On The High Seas")

Music by Jule Styne
Lyric by Sammy Cahn

* Letter A, bars 15 & 16, are originally:

Johnny One Note
(from "Babes In Arms")

Music by Richard Rodgers
Lyric by Lorenz Hart

Just One Of Those Things
(from "Jubilee")

Cole Porter

Solo on ABC
After solos, D.S. al fine

* Bars 13-16 of letter A are sometimes played:

The Lady Is A Tramp

(from "Babes In Arms")

Music by Richard Rodgers
Lyric by Lorenz Hart

Lester Leaps In

Lester Young

Bright

The melody is sometimes played:

(etc.)

YUSEF LATEEF, CANNONBALL ADDERLEY & NAT ADDERLEY

Photo by Jim Marshall

Let's Call The Whole Thing Off

(from "Shall We Dance?")

George Gershwin
Ira Gershwin

Solo on ABC
After solos, D.S. al fine

Let's Do It (Let's Fall In Love)

(from "Paris")

Cole Porter

ADDITIONAL REFRAINS:

The nightingales, in the dark do it,
Larks, k-razy for a lark, do it,
Let's do it, Let's fall in love.
Canaries, caged in the house, do it,
When they're out of season, grouse do it,
Let's do it, Let's fall in love.
The most sedate barnyard fowls do it,
When a chanticleer cries,
High-browed old owls do it,
They're supposed to be wise,
Penguins in flocks, on the rocks, do it,
Even little cuckoos, in their clocks, do it,
Let's do it, Let's fall in love.

Romantic sponges, they say, do it,
Oysters, down in Oyster Bay, do it,
Let's do it, Let's fall in love.
Cold Cape Cod clams, 'gainst their wish, do it,
Even lazy Jellyfish do it,
Let's do it, Let's fall in love.
Electric eels, I might add, do it,
Though it shocks 'em I know.
Why ask if shad do it,
Waiter, bring me shadroe.
In shallow shoals, English soles do it,
Goldfish, in the privacy of bowls, do it,
Let's do it, Let's fall in love.

The dragonflies, in the reeds, do it,
Sentimental centipedes do it,
Let's do it, Let's fall in love.
Mosquitoes, heaven forbid, do it,
So does ev'ry katydid, do it,
Let's do it, Let's fall in love.
The most refined lady bugs do it,
When a gentleman calls,
Moths in your rugs, do it,
What's the use of moth balls?
Locusts in trees do it, bees do it,
Even overeducated fleas do it,
Let's do it, Let's fall in love.

The chimpanzees, in the zoos, do it,
Some courageous kangaroos do it,
Let's do it, Let's fall in love.
I'm sure giraffes, on the sly, do it,
Heavy hippopotami do it,
Let's do it, Let's fall in love.
Old sloths who hang down from twigs do it,
Though the effort is great,
Sweet guinea pigs do it,
Buy a couple and wait.
The world admits bears in pits do it,
Even pekineses in the Ritz, do it,
Let's do it, Let's fall in love.

273

Li'l Darlin'

Neal Hefti

In the original Basie version, the solo is letter E only (16 bars) with the D.C. at the end of letter E.

A Lot Of Livin' To Do

(fron "Bye Bye Birdie")

Music by Charles Strouse
Lyric by Lee Adams

276

Love For Sale

(from "The New Yorkers")

Cole Porter

The ending is extended in the original sheet music.
The first 8 bars of letters A, B, and D are sometimes played with all major or all minor chords.

Love Is A Many Splendored Thing

(from "Love Is A Many Splendored Thing")

Music by Sammy Fain
Lyric by Paul Francis Webster
(As performed by Keith Jarrett)

* Keith Jarrett performs this at a Bright Tempo, omitting the verse.

The main chords are Keith Jarrett's basic chords. The alternates are primarily the original changes.
* Originally

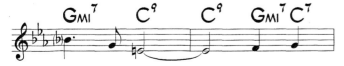

Solo on AB
After solos, D.S. al fine

Love Me Or Leave Me

(from "Whoopee!")

Music by Walter Donaldson
Lyric by Gus Kahn

give back to-mor - row; For my love is your love, there's no love for no-bod-y else!

Love Speaks Louder Than Words

Bill Champlin, Richard Feldman
& Glenn Friedman
(As performed by Al Jarreau)

You and I, stalk-in' each oth - er, beat-in' a-round the bush.
Ev-'ry time you make a pro - mise, I've been the one who waits.

You and I, stuck in the weath - er, some-bod-y needs a push.
And the time's keep-in' it from us. Love nev-er comes too late.

Ev-'ry time you de-cide that the time is-n't right, ev-'ry time that you hide From your
As I live and I breathe you will some - day be-lieve I'm the one that you need. Let your

feel-in's your lone-li-ness wins.
feel-in's for - get where you've been. Let love be -

gin. Let the ma-gic hap - pen, Give me half a chance. I

hold you now. I'll show you how I'll give you all of my Love speaks loud-er than words.

On the rhythm part letter A is written as 8 bars repeated.

Love Speaks Louder Than Words (Rhythm Section)

On the main part, letter A is written without a repeat (16 bars).

Love Walked In
(from "The Goldwyn Follies")

George Gershwin
Ira Gershwin

Lover, Come Back To Me

(from "The New Moon")

Music by Sigmund Romberg
Lyric by Oscar Hammerstein II

Solo on ABC
After solos, D.S. al fine

Originally written as follows: (It is almost always performed as in the chart.)

(etc.)

Lucky To Be Me

(from "On The Town")

Music by Leonard Bernstein
Lyric by Betty Comden
and Adolph Green

Some versions use the optional shorter ending each time.
The original ending is correctly used each time.

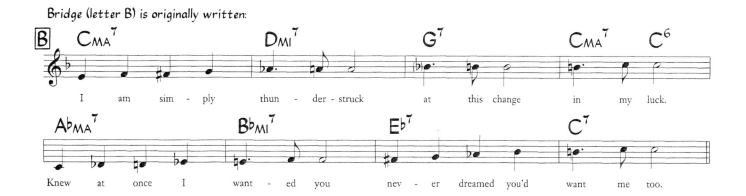

Lullaby Of Broadway

(from "Gold Diggers of 1935")

Music by Harry Warren
Lyric by Al Dubin

294

Milk-man's on his way. Sleep tight, Ba - by.

Sleep tight, Let's call it a day. Hey!

Solo on ABC
After solos, D.S. al Last x ending

Let's call it a day! Lis - ten to the lul - la - by of

Old Broad - way.

* The ending is sometimes extended:

Old Broad - way.

The Man I Love
(from "Lady, Be Good")

George Gershwin
Ira Gershwin

* Also played Up Tempo (Double Time feel).

The Man That Got Away

(from "A Star Is Born")

Music by Harold Arlen
Lyric by Ira Gershwin

Solo on AABC
After solos, D.S. al fine
or take Optional Tag

Portuguese lyric:

Quem acreditou
No amor, no sorriso, na flor
Então sonhou, sonhou...
E perdeu a paz
O amor, o sorriso e a flor
Se transformam depressa demais
Quem, no coração
Abrigou a tristeza de ver
Tudo isto se perder
E, na solidão
Procurou um caminho e seguiu
Já descrente de um dia feliz

Quem chorou, chorou
E tanto que seu pranto já secou

Quem depois voltou
Ao amor, ao sorriso e á flor
Então, tudo encontrou
Pois, a própria dor
Revelou o caminho do amor
E a tristeza acabou

Minute By Minute

Music by Michael McDonald
Lyric by Michael McDonald and Lester Abrams
(As performed by the Doobie Brothers)

Hey, ____ don't wor — ry, ____ I've been lied ____ to.
You ____ would stay just to ____ watch me, dar — lin',

I've ____ been there man — y ____ times be — fore. ____ Girl, don't you
wilt ____ a — way on ____ lies from you. ____ Can't stop the

wor — ry. ____ I know where I stand. ____ I don't need ____ this
hab — it of liv — in' on the run. ____ Take it all ____ for

love. ____ I don't need your hand. ____ I know I ____ could
grant — ed like you're the on — ly one. ____ Liv — in' on ____ my

turn, blink, and you'd be gone. Then I must be ____ pre —
own, some — how that sounds nice. You think I'm ____ your

pared ____ an — y time to car — ry on. But ____
fool. ____ Well, you may just be right. ____ 'Cause ____

min — ute by min — ute by min — ute by min — ute I keep hold — in' on. ____

The recorded version of this song has a longer Intro.
Chords on this main part are simplified. Chords on the rhythm part are more detailed.

Minute By Minute (Rhythm Section)

The recorded version of this song has a longer Intro.

(Vamp & fade)

Miss Otis Regrets
(She's Unable To Lunch Today)
(from "Hi Diddle Diddle")

Cole Porter

* Often performed out of tempo throughout.

Solo on B

Moondance

Van Morrison

The More I See You

(from "Diamond Horseshoe")

Music by Harry Warren
Lyric by Mack Gordon

Solo on ABCD
After solos, D.S. al fine

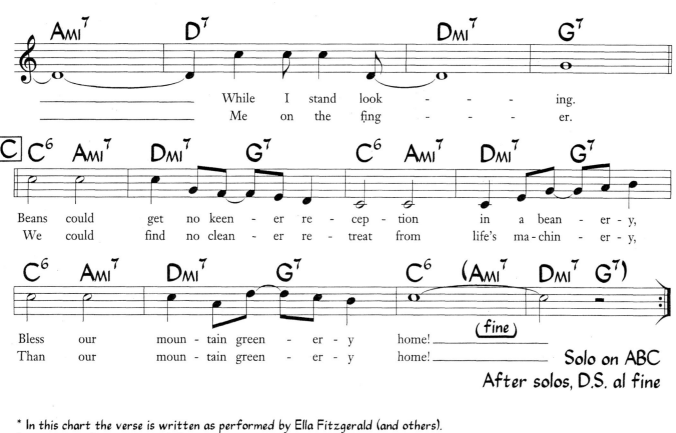

While I stand look - - - ing.
Me on the fing - - - er.

Beans could get no keen - er re - cep - tion in a bean - er - y,
We could find no clean - er re - treat from life's ma - chin - er - y,

Bless our moun - tain green - er - y home! _____ (fine)
Than our moun - tain green - er - y home! _____ Solo on ABC
After solos, D.S. al fine

* In this chart the verse is written as performed by Ella Fitzgerald (and others).
It was originally written as follows:

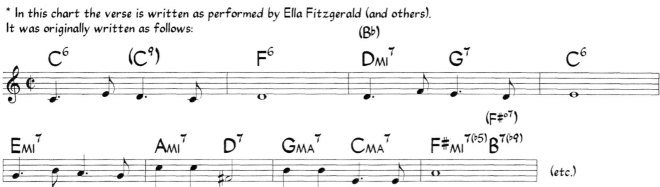

(etc.)

Mr. Lucky
(from "Mr. Lucky")

Music by Henry Mancini
Lyric by Jay Livingston & Ray Evans

Photo by Paul J. Hoeffler, Toronto   **HERBIE HANCOCK**

My Funny Valentine

(from "Babes In Arms")

Music by Richard Rodgers
Lyric by Lorenz Hart

Freely

(Verse)

Be - hold the way our fine - feath-ered friend his vir - tue doth pa -

rade. Thou know - est not, my dim - wit - ted friend, The

pic - ture thou hast made. Thy va - cant brow and thy

tous - led hair con - ceal thy good in - tent. Thou no - ble, up - right,

truth - ful, sin - cere and slight - ly dop - ey gent, you're

*(Ballad or Medium)

A

My fun - ny Val - en - tine, Sweet com - ic Val - en - tine,

You make me smile with my heart. _____

Your looks are laugh - a - ble, Un - pho - to - graph - a - ble,

*This tune has been performed in many styles and tempos, and with many different chord progressions.

My Heart Stood Still

(from "A Connecticut Yankee")

Music by Richard Rodgers
Lyric by Lorenz Hart

* Also performed up tempo.

My Man's Gone Now
(from "Porgy And Bess")

George Gershwin
Ira Gershwin
Du Bose & Dorothy Heyward
(As played by Bill Evans)

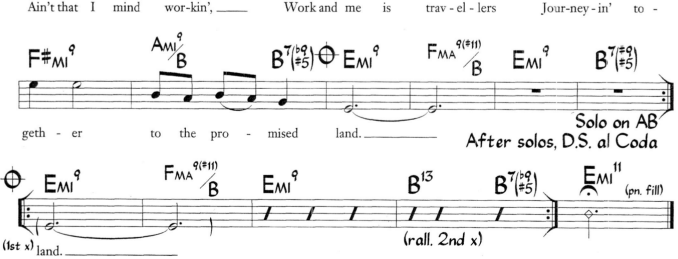

Medium Ballad

(Intro) Emi9 (ad lib) Fma9(#11)/B Emi9 B7(#9)(#5)

A Emi9 Fma9/B Emi9 B13 E7(#9)

My man's gone now, ain't no use a-lis-t'nin' For his tired

Ami9 B7sus(b9) B7(#9)(#5) Emi9 Fma9(#11)/B Emi9 B7(#9)(#5)

foot-steps climb-in' up the stairs.

Emi9 Fma9/B Emi9 B13 E7(#9)

Ole Man Sor-row's come to keep me com-p'ny, Whis-per-in' be-

Ami9 B7sus(b9) B7(#9)(#5) Emi9 Fma9(#11)/B Emi9 B7(#9)(#5)

side me when I say my prayers.

B Bb13 Bb7(#5) EbMA9 Eb6 B13 B9(#5) Emi9 C#13 C#9(#5)

Ain't that I mind wor-kin', Work and me is trav-el-ers Jour-ney-in' to-

F#mi9 Ami9/B B7(b9)(#5) Emi9 Fma9(#11)/B Emi9 B7(#9)(#5)

geth-er to the pro-mised land.

Solo on AB
After solos, D.S. al Coda

Emi9 Fma9(#11)/B Emi9 B13 B7(b9)(#5) Emi11 (pn. fill)

(1st x) land.

(rall. 2nd x)

The original version has additional interludes, repeated sections, and a tag. (The original form is AABBA and Tag.)
(See original music for a more complete version.)
Colloquialisms have been replaced by more common words. ("That" for "Dat", "The" for "De", etc.)

Additional lyric: Letter B 2nd time   Final letter A

But Ole Man Sorrow's   Ole Man Sorrow
Marchin' all the way with me Sittin' by the fireplace
Tellin' me I'm old now   Lyin' all night long
Since I lose my man.   By me in the bed.

Nancy (With The Laughing Face)

Music by James Van Heusen
Lyric by Phil Silvers

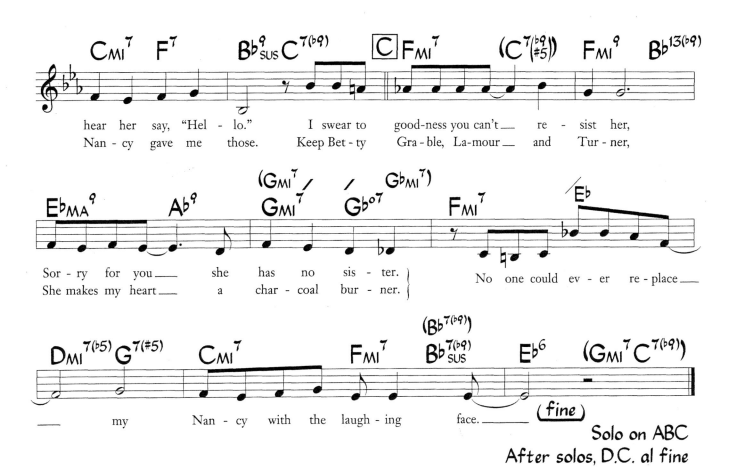

hear her say, "Hel - lo." I swear to good-ness you can't__ re - sist her,
Nan - cy gave me those. Keep Bet - ty Gra - ble, La-mour__ and Tur - ner,

Sor - ry for you__ she has no sis - ter.
She makes my heart__ a char - coal bur - ner.

No one could ev - er re - place__

__ my Nan - cy with the laugh - ing face.__

(fine)
Solo on ABC
After solos, D.C. al fine

Nice Work If You Can Get It

(from "A Damsel In Distress")

George Gershwin
Ira Gershwin

324

Night And Day
(from "The Gay Divorcée")

Cole Porter

326

Not Like This

Photo © Lee Tanner/The Jazz Image

CHET BAKER

Of Thee I Sing

(from "Of Thee I Sing")

George Gershwin
Ira Gershwin

* Also performed Medium or Up Tempo.

Oh, Lady Be Good

(from "Lady, Be Good")

George Gershwin
Ira Gershwin

(The Old Man From)
The Old Country

Nat Adderley
Curtis R. Lewis

Hey, you old man sit - tin' by the lone - some road,
You ain't sired no chil - lun, ain't none by your side,

It's 'bout time you're quit - tin' life's old tire - some load.
You left all your wo - men. Ain't you sa - tis - fied?

You're so sad and lone - ly, got no fam - i - ly.
Don't just sit there cling - in' to a mem - o - ry

Just an old man from some ___ old coun - try. ___
Of a love left in some ___ old coun - try. ___

3rd verse: (Out chorus)

Don't nobody need you, old man,
'Cause nobody calls your name.
Nobody even whispers.
What a dog-gone shame.
So the cold grim reaper
Has no sympathy.
You won't see your homeland
'Cept through me.

Photo by Jerry Stoll

THE JAZZ CELLAR (San Francisco)

Old Folks

Music by Willard Robison
Lyric by Dedette Lee Hill

Lin-coln that day.____
whale got a - way, ____

I know that____ one so well. _____

Don't

quite un - der-stand____ a - bout Old Folks.
some day there'll be_____ no more Old Folks.

Did he fight for the blue____ or the gray? ___
What a lone - ly old town ___ this will be. __

Oh,

For he's so dip - lo - mat - ic and so dem - o - crat - ic,
Chil-dren's voic - es at play___ will be stilled for a day, ___ the
Seems that I've heard some men - tion, he lives on a pen - sion,

we al - ways let him have his way._____
day that they take Old Folks a - way._____
he'll nev - er come right out and say.____

We

Solo on ABC ____

After solos, D.C. al Last ending

(fine)

On A Clear Day
(You Can See Forever)

Music by Burton Lane
Lyric by Alan Jay Lerner

(from "On A Clear Day (You Can See Forever)")

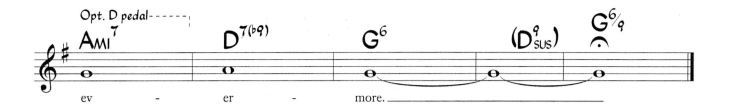

ev - er - more. _____

* Jazz performers most often play and sing as in chart.
Originally written

moun-tain, see and shore. _____

and

nev - er heard be - fore. _____

On A Misty Night

Tadd Dameron

The bridge (letter B) is often played with variations (or ad lib.).

One Hundred Ways

Kathy Wakefield
Benjamin Wright
Tony Coleman

On the original recording the D.S. is only back to letter F.
The instrumental solo is 7 bars, with the vocal entering at the pickups to letter G.

Our Delight

Tadd Dameron

Medium Bright

Bars 7-8 of letter A (and similar spots) are often played as follows:

This piece is often played in D flat.

(Our) Love Is Here To Stay

(from "The Goldwyn Follies")

George Gershwin
Ira Gershwin

Solo on AB
After solos, D.S. al fine

346

People Make The World Go 'Round

Thom Bell
Linda Creed
(as performed by the Stylistics)

348

Piano In The Dark

Brenda Russell, Jeff Hull
and Scott Cutler

(as performed by Brenda Russell)

Piano In The Dark (Rhythm Section)

Pick Up The Pieces

Alan Gorrie, Roger Ball,
Owen McIntyre, Hamish Stuart,
Malcolm Duncan & Robbie McIntosh
(As performed by Average White Band)

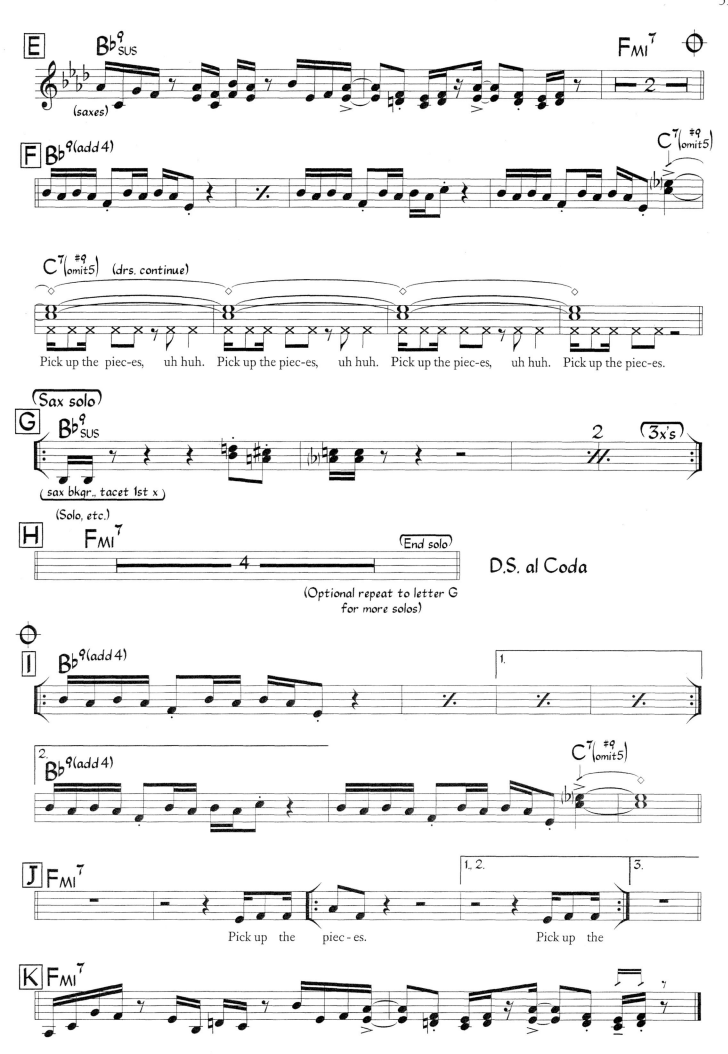

Pick Up The Pieces (Rhythm Section)

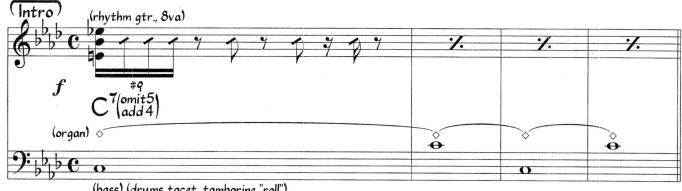

356

Please Don't Talk About Me When I'm Gone

Sidney Clare, Sam H. Stept
& Bee Palmer

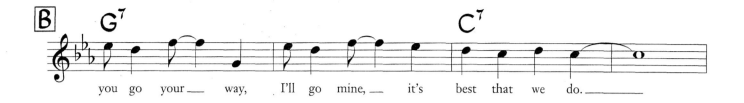

you go your____ way, I'll go mine, ___ it's best that we do._____

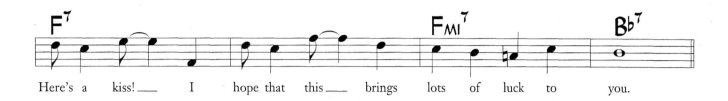

Here's a kiss!____ I hope that this____ brings lots of luck to you.

Makes no diff-'rence how_____ I car - ry on, _____ re - mem - ber,

please don't talk a - bout me when I'm gone. (fine) Solo on ABC
After solos D.S. al fine

Put On A Happy Face
(fron "Bye Bye Birdie")

Music by Charles Strouse
Lyric by Lee Adams

MACHITO & HIS ORCHESTRA

Real Love

Michael McDonald
Patrick Henderson
(As performed by the Doobie Brothers)

Medium Bright Pop

V.S. (turn page)

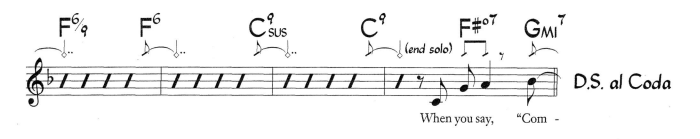

When you say, "Com -

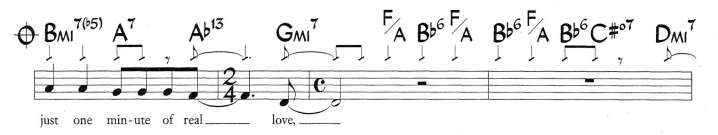

just one min-ute of real____ love, ____

real love, ____   real love. ____

Real love, _____   real love. ____   (Vamp & fade)

Sample bass:

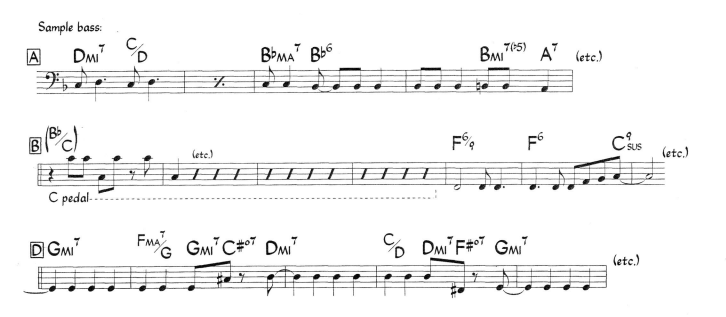

Red Clay
(aka "On The Red Clay")

Music by Freddie Hubbard
Lyric by Mark Murphy

Mark Murphy's lyric to "On The Red Clay":

Screen door slappin' somewhere on the side porch,
A sleepy mornin' way out in the boondocks,
Stories are bein' told on the red clay.

Red clay's where we came from to begin with
And where we're goin' when time comes for splittin'.
Sounds are bein' dug on the red clay.

Movin', always groovin'.
Mornin', midnight, sleep tight.

Someone's playin' somethin' on the back step.
The happy faces look out of the windows.
Always is somethin' good on the red clay.

Waitin' for the paper in the evenin',
You watch the roses climb out of their earth beds.
Life is bein' lived on the red clay.

Smoothin' down my baby when she's tired out.
I tell her fun things and watch her start smilin'.
Nobody bein' sad on my red clay.

Your move, my move, check me.
He moves, they move, dig me?

Red clay's just the dirt, but it's alive, son.
So what you doin' just sittin' there goofin'?
Always a lot to do on the red clay.

Rockin' In Rhythm

Duke Ellington
Irving Mills
Harry Carney

'Round Midnight

Music by Thelonious Monk
& Cootie Williams
Lyric by Bernie Hanighen

There are many different versions of this tune. The Intro, Interlude and "Last x" ending are optional.

'S Wonderful
(from "Funny Face")

George Gershwin
Ira Gershwin

Sabiá
(Song Of The Sabiá)

Music by Antonio Carlos Jobim
Portuguese Lyric by Chico Buarque
English lyric by Norman Gimbel

someone's love will speed the night, the lonely unwanted night that may bring me to the new day. I'll go back. I know now that I'll go back. They were not in vain, All the plans I made to deceive myself, All the roads I made just to lose myself, All the love I made to forget myself, All mistakes I made just to find myself. _(fine)_ (I'll go back, ___)

Solo on ABC
After solos, D.C. al fine

*Cedar Walton plays this with a jazz feel in 2 (for the head).

(Portuguese lyric)

Vou voltar, Sei que ainda, vou voltar.
Para o meu lugar Foi lá
E é, ainda, lá, Que eu hei de ouvir cantar
Uma sabiá, Cantar uma sabiá.

Vou voltar, Sei que ainda, vou voltar.
Vou deitar à sombra de uma palmeira
Que já não dá, Colher a flor que já não dá,
E algum amor Talvez, possa espantar
As noites que eu não queria
E anunciar o dia.

Vou voltar, Sei que ainda, vou voltar.
Não vai ser em vão,
Que fiz tantos planos de me enganar,
Como fiz enganos de me encontrar,
Come fiz estradas de me peridr,
Fiz de tudo e nada de te exquecer.

Saving All My Love For You

Music by Michael Masser
Lyric by Gerry Goffin
(as performed by Whitney Houston)

(Optional D.S. al Coda)

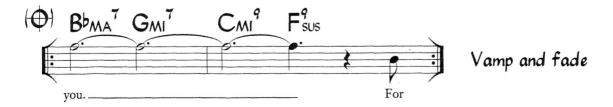

Vamp and fade

Secret Love

Music by Sammy Fain
Lyric by Paul Francis Webster

* Also performed Up Tempo.

The last 4 bars (plus the pick-up) are sometimes played or sung as follows:

Bars 1-14 and 17-28 of letter A are often played over a B-flat pedal.

September In The Rain

(from "Gold Diggers of 1935")

Music by Harry Warren
Lyric by Al Dubin

rain - drops seemed to play a sweet re - frain._____ Though

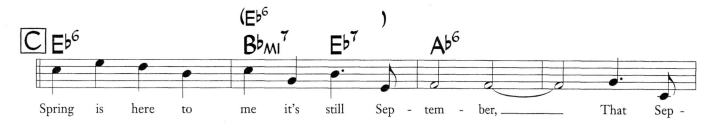

Spring is here to me it's still Sep - tem - ber,_____ That Sep -

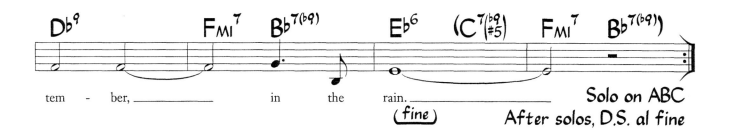

tem - ber,_____ in the rain._____ Solo on ABC

(fine)   After solos, D.S. al fine

Alternate chords for letter A, bars 1-2 & 9-10, and letter C, bars 1-2:

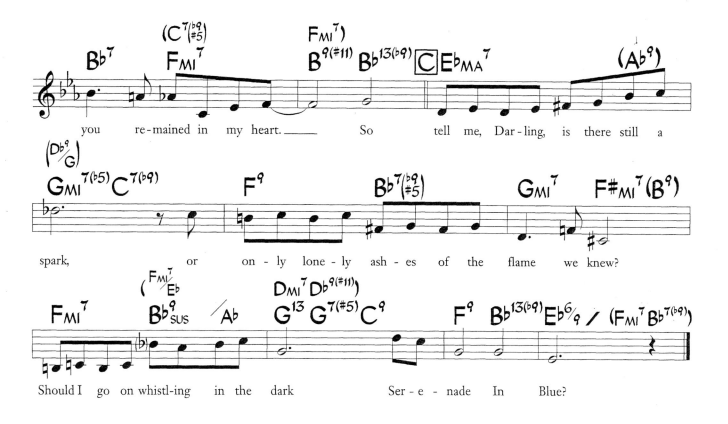

you re-mained in my heart._____ So tell me, Dar - ling, is there still a

spark, or on - ly lone - ly ash - es of the flame we knew?

Should I go on whistl-ing in the dark Ser - e - nade In Blue?

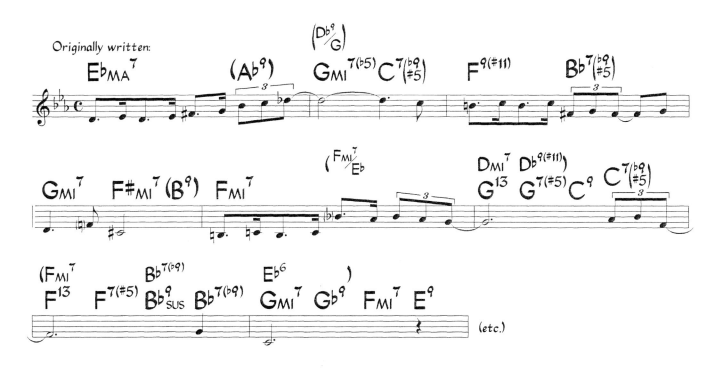

Originally written:

(etc.)

Shiny Stockings

Music by Frank Foster
Lyric by Ella Fitzgerald

She: Those silk shin-y stock-ings that I wear when I'm with you, ___ I
He: Those silk shin-y stock-ings that you wear when I'm with you, ___ You

wear 'cause you told ___ me that you dig that cra-zy hue. ___ Do
wear 'cause I told ___ you that I dig that cra-zy hue. ___ When

we think of ro-mance ___ When we go to a dance? ___ Oh, no, ___
we go to a dance ___ Do I think of ro-mance? ___ No, all ___

___ You take a glance ___ at those shin - y silk stock - ings.
___ I do is glance ___ at those shin - y silk stock - ings.

Then came a - long ___ some chick with great big stock-ings too. ___ When
Then came a - long ___ some guy who dug your stock-ings too. ___ When

you changed your mind ___ a - bout me; why I nev - er knew. ___ I
you changed your mind ___ a - bout me; why I nev - er knew. ___ I

guess I'll have to find ___ a new, a ___ new kind; ___ A
guess I'll have to find ___ a new, a ___ new kind; ___ A

guy who digs my shin - y stock-ings too. ___
gal who wears those shin - y stock-ings too. ___

Solo on AB
After solos, go on
or D.C. al Coda

Till cue / On cue
Solo on AB
(ens.) *mp*

A new guy___ who digs my shin - y stock-ings too.___
A new gal___ who digs my shin - y stock-ings too.___ (pn. 8va b.)

(top note of chord)

In Ella Fitzgerald's version the 1st ending of letter D is omitted. The D.S. al Coda is taken.

Since I Fell For You

Buddy Johnson

Often performed in F.

Slow Hot Wind

Music by Henry Mancini
Lyric by Norman Gimbel

Photo © Lee Tanner/The Jazz Image

ELLA FITZGERALD

So In Love

(from "Kiss Me Kate")

Cole Porter

*Also performed as a Samba or Bossa Nova

So Nice (Summer Samba)
(Samba De Verão)

Music and Portuguese Lyric by
Marcos Valle & Paulo Sergio Valle
English lyric by Norman Gimbel

Medium Bossa Nova

A | FMA⁹ | BMI⁷

Some-one to hold me tight, that would be ve-ry nice. Some-one to love me right,

E⁷⁽♯⁵⁾ | B♭MA⁹ | B♭⁶/₉

that would be ve-ry nice. Some-one to un-der-stand each lit-tle dream __ in me,

E♭⁹ | **B** AMI⁷

some-one to take my hand, to be a team __ with me. So nice, __

D⁷⁽♭⁹⁾⁽♯⁵⁾ | GMI⁷ | EMI⁷⁽♭⁵⁾ A⁷⁽♯⁵⁾ | DMI⁹

__ life would be so nice __ if one day I'd find __

G¹³ | GMI⁷ | D♭⁹ C⁹

__ some-one who would take my hand and sam-ba thru life __ with me.

C FMA⁹ | BMI⁷

Some-one to cling to me, stay with me right __ or wrong, some-one to sing to me

E⁷⁽♯⁵⁾ | B♭MA⁹ | B♭⁶/₉

some lit-tle sam - ba song. Some-one to take my heart, then give his heart __ to me.

E♭⁹ | **D** AMI⁷

Some-one who's read-y to give love a start __ with me. Oh yes, __

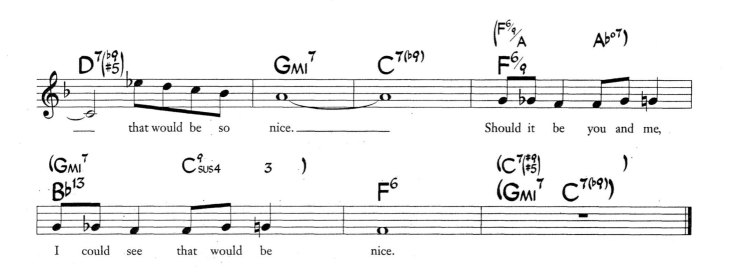

that would be so nice. _____ Should it be you and me,

I could see that would be nice.

Softly, As In A Morning Sunrise
(from "New Moon")

Music by Sigmund Romberg
Lyric by Oscar Hammerstein II

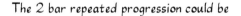

* Originally a Tango

Some Other Time

Music by Leonard Bernstein
Lyric by Betty Comden
& Adolph Green
(As played by Bill Evans)

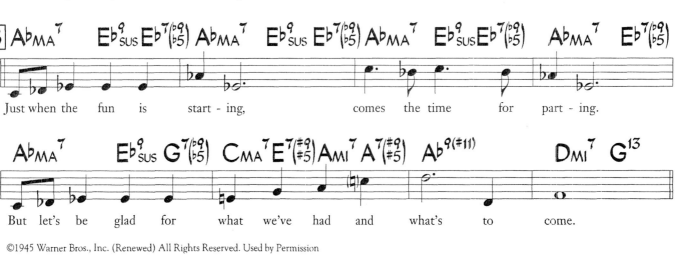

Twen-ty-four hours can go so fast, you look a-round, the day has passed.

When you're in love time is pre-cious stuff; E-ven a life-time is-n't e-nough!

Where has the time all gone to? Have-n't done half the things we want to.

Oh, well, we'll catch up some oth-er time.

This day was just a to-ken, Too man-y words are still un-spo-ken.

Oh, well, we'll catch up some oth-er time.

Just when the fun is start-ing, comes the time for part-ing.

But let's be glad for what we've had and what's to come.

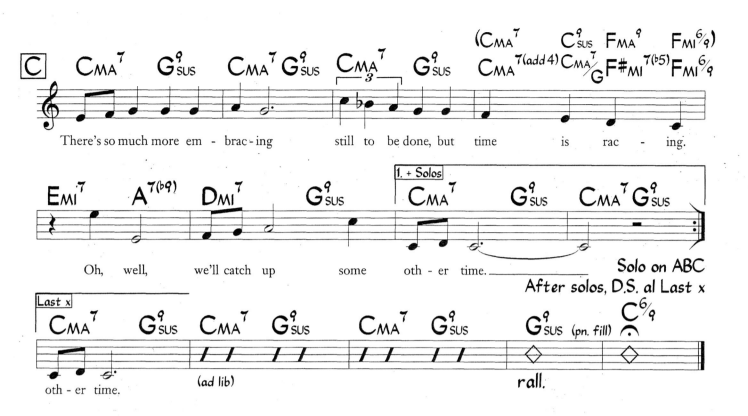

There's so much more em - brac - ing   still to be done, but   time   is   rac - ing.

Oh,   well,   we'll catch up   some   oth - er time._____   Solo on ABC

After solos, D.S. al Last x

oth - er time.   (ad lib)   rall.

* Bill Evans did not play the verse. He played a 4 bar Intro:

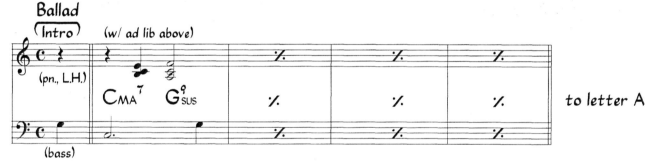

to letter A

Somebody Loves Me

(from "George White's Scandals of 1924")

George Gershwin
Ira Gershwin

Medium or Freely

(Verse) Emi F#mi/B Emi A/E Emi F#mi/B Emi A/E

When this world be-gan   It was Heav-en's plan,

F#mi7(b5) B7(b9) Emi7 C#mi7(b5) C9(#11) B7(b9)(#5) Emi6

There should be a girl for ev-'ry sin-gle man.

G6 Ami/G G6 G6 Ami/G G6

To my great re-gret,   Some-one has up-set

Ami7 D7 Gma7 G7 Eb9(b5) D13(b9) Emi Emi6

Heav-en's pret-ty pro-gram for we've nev-er met.   I'm

Bmi Bmi7 E7 Emi7 *poco rit.* A7 D9sus D7(b9)

clutch-ing at straws, just be-cause I may meet her yet.

Med. Ballad or Medium

[A] Gma7 (Emi7) Ami7 D7(b9) Gma7 (C9) Eb9

Some-bod-y loves me,   I won-der who,

Gma7 (Emi7) (Eb9) A7(b9) D9sus D7(b9) G6 (E7) Ami7 D7(b9)

I won-der who { she he } can be. _____

Gma7 (Emi7) Ami7 D7(b9) Gma7 (Emi6) C#mi7(b5) (F#7(b9))

Some-bod-y loves me,   I wish I knew,

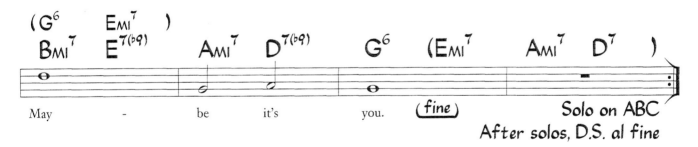

Bars 1-2 and 9-10 of letter A and bars 1-2 of letter C are most often performed by jazz musicians as in the main chart. They were originally written as follows:

Someone To Watch Over Me

(from "Oh, Kay")

George Gershwin
Ira Gershwin

400

This was originally a Medium (or Up) Tempo tune.
Traditionally it is more often performed as a Ballad, often with even eighth notes.

Something To Talk About

Shirley Eikhard
(As performed by Bonnie Raitt)

Med. Country Rock

(acous. gtr.)
(bkgr. vocals) Ooh, _____   ooh, _____   ooh, __
(el. gtr. solo)

All Rhythm in

A
Peo-ple are talk-in',   talk-in' 'bout peo-ple. __   I hear them whis-per,
I feel so fool-ish,   I nev-er no-ticed __   you'd act so ner-vous.

You won't be-lieve it.   They think we're lov-ers   kept un-der-co-ver_____
Could you be fall-in' for me?   It took a ru-mor   to make me won-der. __

I'll just ig-nore it,   but they keep say-in' we   **B** laugh __ just a lit-tle too loud, __
Now __ I'm con-vinced I'm __   go-in' un-der.   Think-in' 'bout you ev-er-y day, __

__ stand _____ just a lit-tle too close. __   We stare _____ just a lit-tle too long. __
__ dream-in' 'bout you ev-'ry night. __   I'm hop-in' that you feel the same way. __

crescendo
May-be they're see-in'   some-thin we don't, __ dar-lin'.
Now that we know it,   let's real-ly show it, dar-lin',

C
Let's give 'em some-thing to talk a-bout.   Let's give 'em some-thing to talk a-bout.
Let's give 'em some-thing to talk a-bout;   A lit-tle mys-t'ry to fig-ure out.

There are background vocal parts on the original Bonnie Raitt recording not on this chart.

Something To Talk About (Rhythm Section)

Med. Country Rock

Sometimes I'm Happy

(from "Hit The Deck")

Music by Vincent Youmans
Lyric by Irving Caesar
and Clifford Grey

* Originally written:
Letter A, bars 11-12 and letter B, bars 11-12;

** Originally written:
Letter A, bars 14-16;

A Song For You

Leon Russell

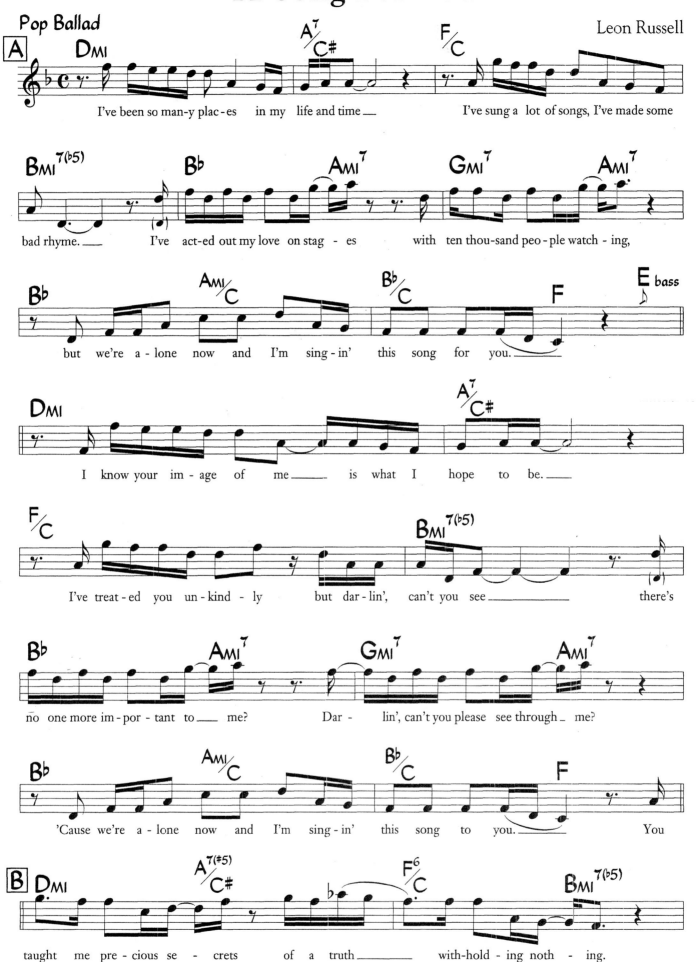

Pop Ballad

I've been so man-y plac-es in my life and time __ I've sung a lot of songs, I've made some bad rhyme. __ I've act-ed out my love on stag - es with ten thou-sand peo - ple watch - ing, but we're a - lone now and I'm sing - in' this song for you. __ I know your im - age of me __ is what I hope to be. __ I've treat-ed you un-kind - ly but dar - lin', can't you see __ there's no one more im - por - tant to __ me? Dar - lin', can't you please see through __ me? 'Cause we're a - lone now and I'm sing - in' this song to you. __ You taught me pre - cious se - crets of a truth __ with-hold - ing noth - ing.

* Leon Russell inserts 2 bars before going on to letter C.

Soon

(from "Strike Up The Band")

George Gershwin
Ira Gershwin

B Eᵇ MA⁷ (Aᵇ MA⁹) G MI⁷⁽ᵇ⁵⁾ (Dᵇ⁷) C⁷⁽♯⁵⁾ C⁷

soon_____ a lit - tle cot - tage will find us
soon_____ our lit - tle ship will come sail - ing

F MI⁷ (Aᵇ MI⁷ Dᵇ⁷) F MI⁷⁽ᵇ⁵⁾ Bᵇ⁷⁽♯⁵⁾ Bᵇ⁷ B⁷ Bᵇ⁷

safe_____ with all our cares far be - hind us.
home_____ through ev - 'ry storm, nev - er fail - ing.

Eᵇ MA⁷ Bᵇ MI⁷ Eᵇ⁷ *Aᵇ MA⁷⁽ᵃᵈᵈ⁶⁾ Dᵇ⁹

The day you're mine this world will be in tune.

(Eᵇ MA⁷/Bᵇ) (Aᵇ MI⁶/Bᵇ) (Eᵇ⁶/Bᵇ) (Aᵇ MI⁶/Bᵇ)
G MI⁷ C MI⁷ F MI⁷ Bᵇ¹³⁽ᵇ⁹⁾ Eᵇ⁶ (F MI⁷ Bᵇ⁷)

Let's make that day come soon._____

(fine)

Solo on AB
After solos, D.S. al fine

* Originally

Soul Man

Isaac Hayes
David Porter
(As performed by Sam & Dave)

Medium Soul Rock

1. to you on a dust-y road. ___ Good lov-in', I got a
2. what I got the hard ___ way ___ and I'll make it bet-ter each and
3. brought up on a side street. ___ I learned how to love be-

truck-load. ___ And when you get it you got ___ some-thin', So
ev-'ry day. ___ So, ___ ho-ney, don't you fret, ___ 'cause
fore I could eat. I was ed-u-ca-ted at Wood-stock. ___ When

don't ___ wor-ry 'cause I'm ___ com-in.' I'm a soul man. ___
you ain't seen noth-in' yet. I'm a soul man. ___
I start lov-in' I can't stop.

I'm a soul man. ___ I'm a soul man. ___ I'm a

413

Stormy Weather
(Keeps Raining All The Time)

Music by Harold Arlen
Lyric by Ted Koehler

(from "Cotton Club Parade - 22nd Edition")

414

* Originally written with a 2-bar extension before letter B (as follows):

Originally written:

The Interlude is usually omitted from jazz (and other) versions.

Strike Up The Band

(from "Strike Up The Band")

George Gershwin
Ira Gershwin

Solo on ABC
After solos, D.S. al fine

Stuck On You

Lionel Richie

* Often melody notes (vocal and instrumental) do not fit the basic written chord.

Suite: Judy Blue Eyes

Stephen Stills
(As performed by Crosby, Stills & Nash)

V.S. (turn page)

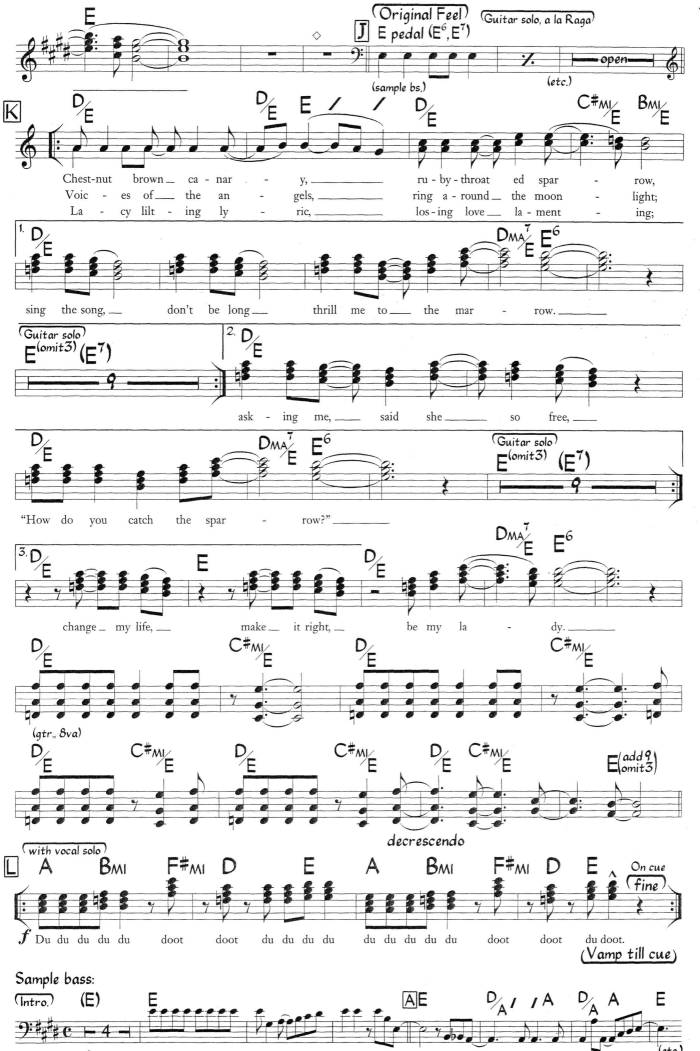

The Summer Knows
(Theme from "Summer of '42)

Music by Michel Legrand
Lyric by Marilyn Bergman
& Alan Bergman

her to tell, One last ca - ress, _____ it's time to dress for

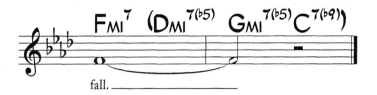

fall. _____

Summer Night

Music by Harry Warren
Lyric by Al Dubin

426

Bars 5 & 6 of letters A and B are often performed

Also performed as a waltz (Ballad or Medium).

Summertime

(from "Porgy and Bess")

George Gershwin
Ira Gershwin
Du Bose & Dorothy Heyward

Background from Miles Davis' "Porgy and Bess" recording (originally in B♭):

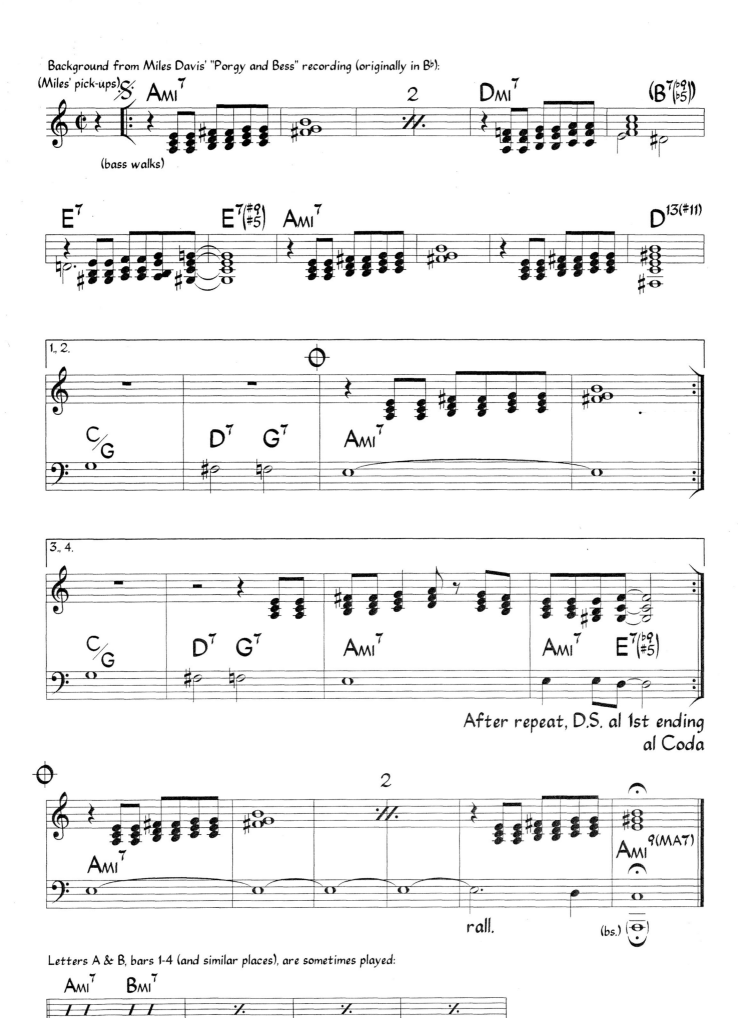

After repeat, D.S. al 1st ending al Coda

rall.

(bs.)

Letters A & B, bars 1-4 (and similar places), are sometimes played:

Sunny

Bobby Hebb

Additional verses:

Sunny, thank you for the truth you let me see.
Sunny, thank you for the facts from A to Z.
My life was torn like wind-blown sand,
Then a rock was formed when we held hands.
Sunny one so true, I love you.

Sunny, thank you for that smile upon your face.
Sunny, thank you for that gleam that flows with grace.
You're my spark of nature's fire,
You're my sweet complete desire.
Sunny one so true, I love you.

The melody is also played or sung as follows:

Photo © Lee Tanner/The Jazz Image

ARETHA FRANKLIN

Sure Enough

John Lang, Richard Page
Steve George and Susan George
(As performed by Tom Scott)

Sure Enough (Rhythm Section)

(Vamp (with fills) and fade)

Sweet Georgia Brown

Ben Bernie
Maceo Pinkard
Kenneth Casey

Solo on AB
After solos, D.S. al fine

Originally written

(etc.)

* Optional chords for the last 4 bars of letter A:

Originally written in the key of G.

Take Five

Paul Desmond
(As played by Dave Brubeck)

438

Takin' It To The Streets

Michael McDonald
(As performed by the Doobie Brothers)

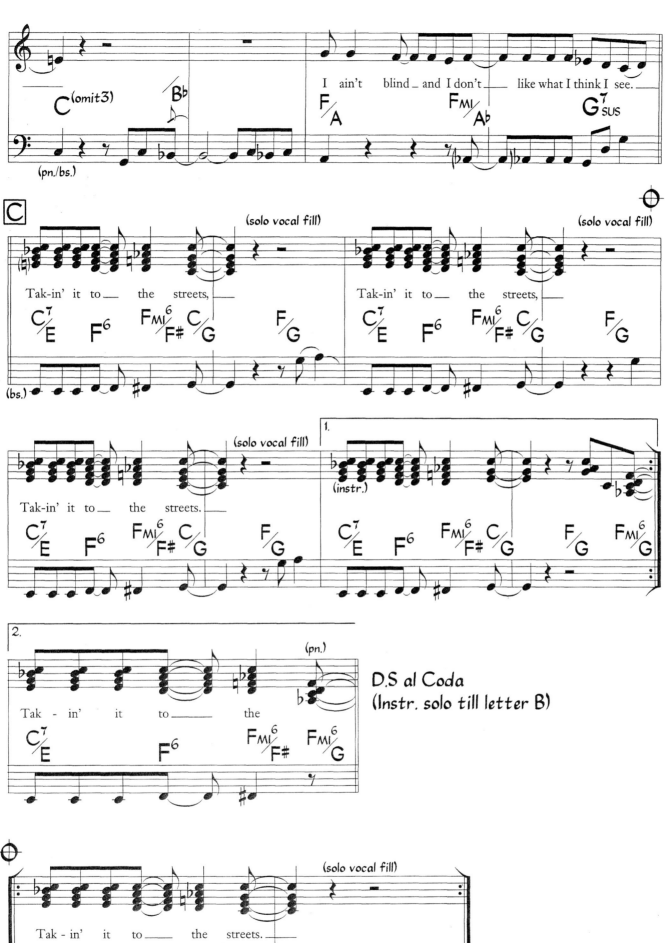

I ain't blind ___ and I don't ___ like what I think I see.

C(omit3)   Bb   F/A   FMI/Ab   G7SUS

(pn./bs.)

C

(solo vocal fill)   (solo vocal fill)

Tak-in' it to ___ the streets, ___   Tak-in' it to ___ the streets, ___

C7/E   F6   FMI6/F#   C/G   F/G   C7/E   F6   FMI6/F#   C/G   F/G

(bs.)

(solo vocal fill)

Tak-in' it to ___ the streets. ___

C7/E   F6   FMI6/F#   C/G   F/G

1.

(instr.)

C7/E   F6   FMI6/F#   C/G   F/G   FMI6/G

2.

Tak - in' it to ___ the

(pn.)

C7/E   F6   FMI6/F#   FMI6/G

D.S al Coda
(Instr. solo till letter B)

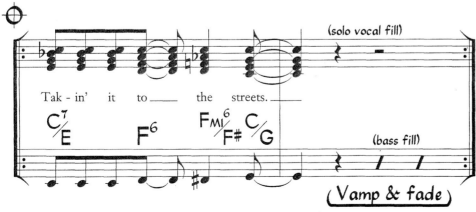

(solo vocal fill)

Tak - in' it to ___ the streets. ___

C7/E   F6   FMI6/F#   C/G

(bass fill)

(Vamp & fade)

Tea For Two

Music by Vincent Youmans
Lyric by Irving Caesar

* Also frequently a Cha Cha.

week - end va - ca - tions, We won't have it known, dear, that we own a tel - e -

phone, dear. Day will break and you'll a - wake and

start to bake a sug - ar cake For me to take for all the boys to

see. _____ We will raise a fam - i - ly, A

boy for you, A girl for me. (Oh,) can't you see how hap - py we would

be. (fine) Solo on ABCD
After solos, D.S. al fine

Alternate changes: Letter D, bars 1-4:

Teach Me Tonight

Music by Gene DePaul
Lyric by Sammy Cahn

near, my love? _____ Grad - u - a - tion's al - most here, my love.

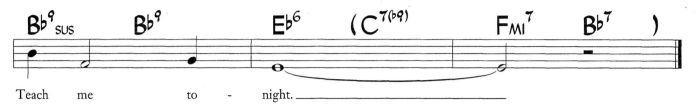

Teach me to - night. _____

The melody is more commonly performed:

Did you say I've got a lot to learn? Well, don't think I'm try - ing

(etc.)

not to learn. _____

That Certain Feeling

(from "Tip Toes")

George Gershwin
Ira Gershwin

(If I Had To Choose)
That Sunday (That Summer)

Joe Sherman
George David Weiss

448

Dar-ling, it would be when you smiled at me that way_____ That

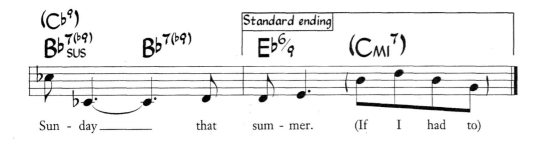

Sun - day_____ that sum - mer. (If I had to)

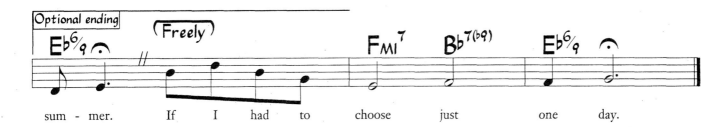

sum - mer. If I had to choose just one day.

That's What Friends Are For

Burt Bacharach
Carole Bayer Sager

450

For good __ times   and bad __ times }   I'll   be   on __   your   side   for - ev   -   er
In good __ times,   in   bad __ times }

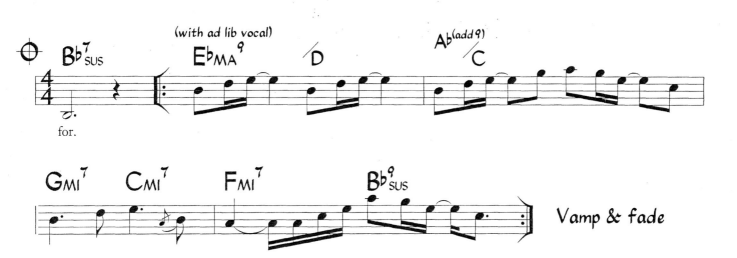

more.   That's what friends __   are   for.   for.   D.S. al Coda

(with ad lib vocal)

for.

Vamp & fade

Then I'll Be Tired Of You

Music by Arthur Schwartz
Lyric by E.Y. "Yip" Harburg

you._____ Be-yond the years_____ Till day is night, Till wrong is right, Till birds re -

fuse to sing, Be - yond the years_____ the ech - o

of my on - ly love will still be whis - per - ing, whis - per - ing.

If my throb - bing heart_____ should ev - er start re - peat - ing

That it is tired of beat - ing Then I'll be tired of

you. (fine) Solo on ABC
After solos, D.S. al fine

Bars 5-8 of letter A are originally harmonized more like this:

There's A Small Hotel
(from "On Your Toes")

Music by Richard Rodgers
Lyric by Lorenz Hart

454

There's No You

Music by Hal Hopper
Lyric by Tom Adair

kiss and re-cap-ture the sum-mer-time rap - ture we knew,___ And from that

day, nev - er more___ will I say___ there's no you. (fine) (I)

Solo on A B C
after solos, D.S. al fine

They All Laughed
(from "Shall We Dance")

George Gershwin
Ira Gershwin

They Can't Take That Away From Me

(from "Shall We Dance")

George Gershwin
Ira Gershwin

Solo on ABC
After solos, D.S. al fine

This Heart Of Mine

(from "Ziegfield Follies")

Music by Harry Warren
Lyric by Arthur Freed

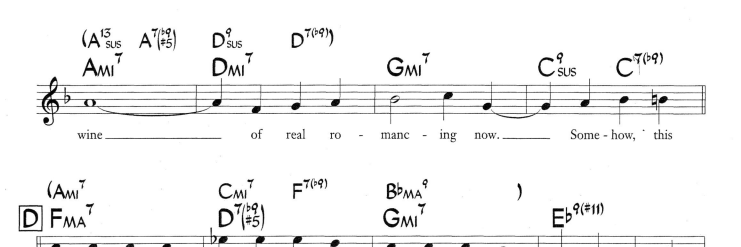

wine _____ of real ro - manc - ing now. _____ Some - how, this

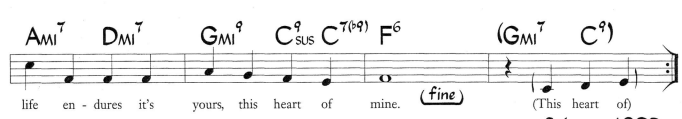

cra - zy world has ta - ken on a won - der - ful de - sign. As long as

life en - dures it's yours, this heart of mine. (*fine*) (This heart of)

Solo on ABCD
After solos, D.S. al fine

This Is Always
(from "Three Little Girls In Blue")

Music by Harry Warren
Lyric by Mack Gordon

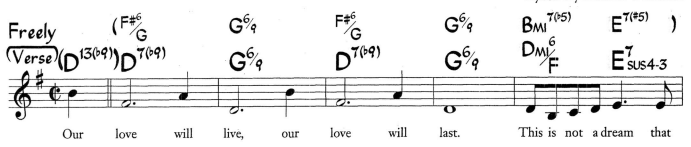

Our love will live, our love will last. This is not a dream that

end - ed with the dawn, It's one that fate in - ten - ded to go on and on.

This is - n't some-times, this is al - ways. This is - n't may-be, this is al -

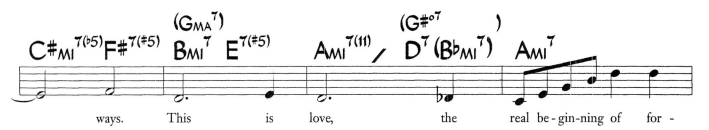

ways. This is love, the real be - gin-ning of for -

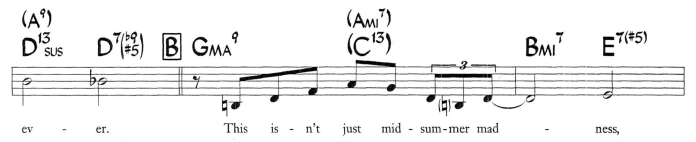

ev - er. This is - n't just mid - sum-mer mad - ness,

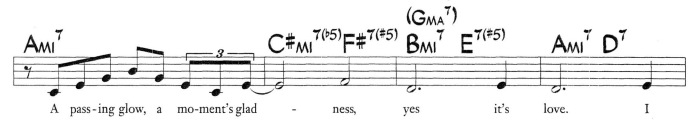

A pass-ing glow, a mo-ment's glad - ness, yes it's love. I

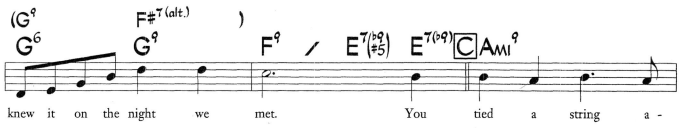

knew it on the night we met. You tied a string a -

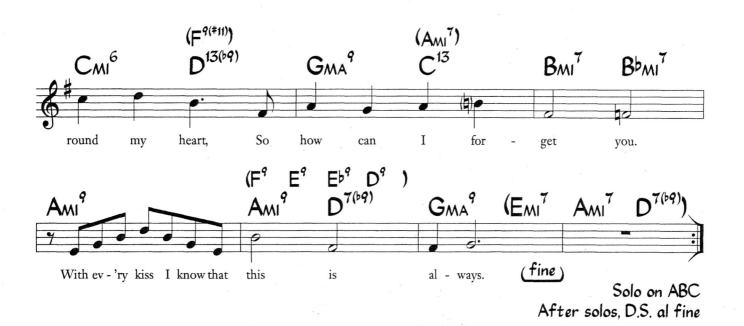

round my heart, So how can I for - get you.

With ev-'ry kiss I know that this is al - ways. (fine)

Solo on ABC
After solos, D.S. al fine

Those Eyes
(Verão)

Music and Portuguese Lyric by
Rosa Passos and Fernando De Oliveira
English Lyric by Brock Walsh
(As performed by Kenny Rankin)

* On Rosa Passo's original version these measures are performed as follows.

This is a slightly condensed version of the Kenny Rankin recording.
Kenny Rankin interprets the melody quite freely.

Thou Swell
(from "A Connecticut Yankee")

Music by Richard Rodgers
Lyric by Lorenz Hart

Solo on AB
After solos, D.S. al fine

Through The Fire

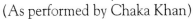

David Foster, Tom P. Keane
& Cynthia Weil

(As performed by Chaka Khan)

Through The Fire (Rhythm Section)

Time After Time

(from "It Happened In Brooklyn")

Music by Jule Styne
Lyric by Sammy Cahn

474

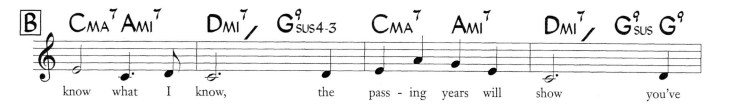

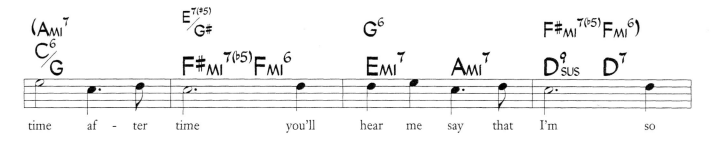

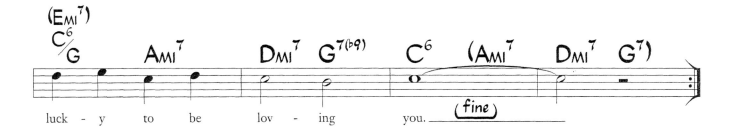

A Time For Love

(from "An American Dream")

Music by Johnny Mandel
Lyric by Paul Francis Webster

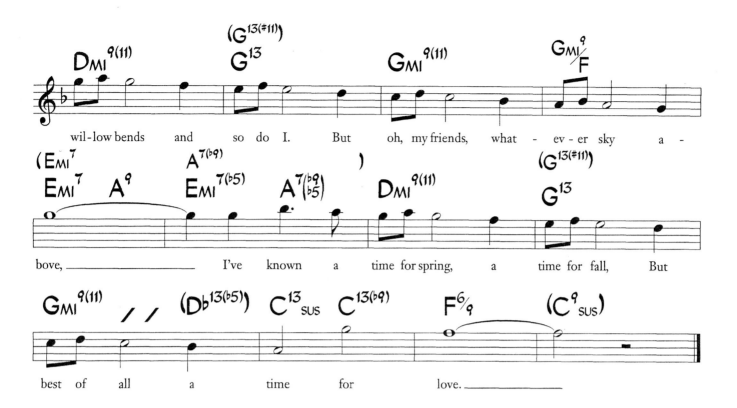

wil-low bends and so do I. But oh, my friends, what - ev - er sky a -

bove, _____ I've known a time for spring, a time for fall, But

best of all a time for love. _____

Time On My Hands
(You In My Arms)

Music by Vincent Youmans
Lyric by Harold Adamson
& Mack Gordon

Solo on ABC
After solos, D.S. al fine

'Tis Autumn

Henry Nemo

Solo on ABC
After solos, D.S. al fine

* Originally written

birds,   the   trees   and   Ole

Letter A, bars 1 & 9, and letter C, bar 1, were originally written:

Tokyo Blues

Horace Silver

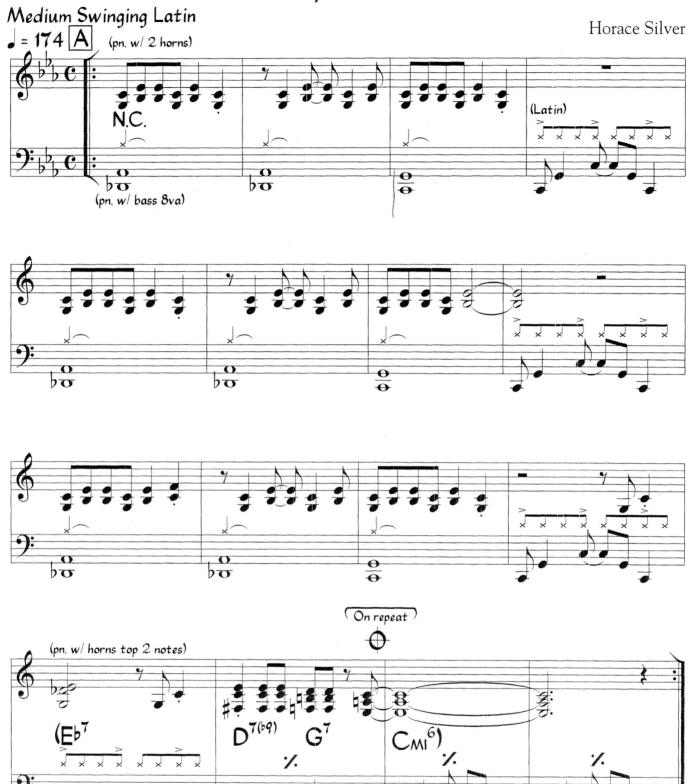

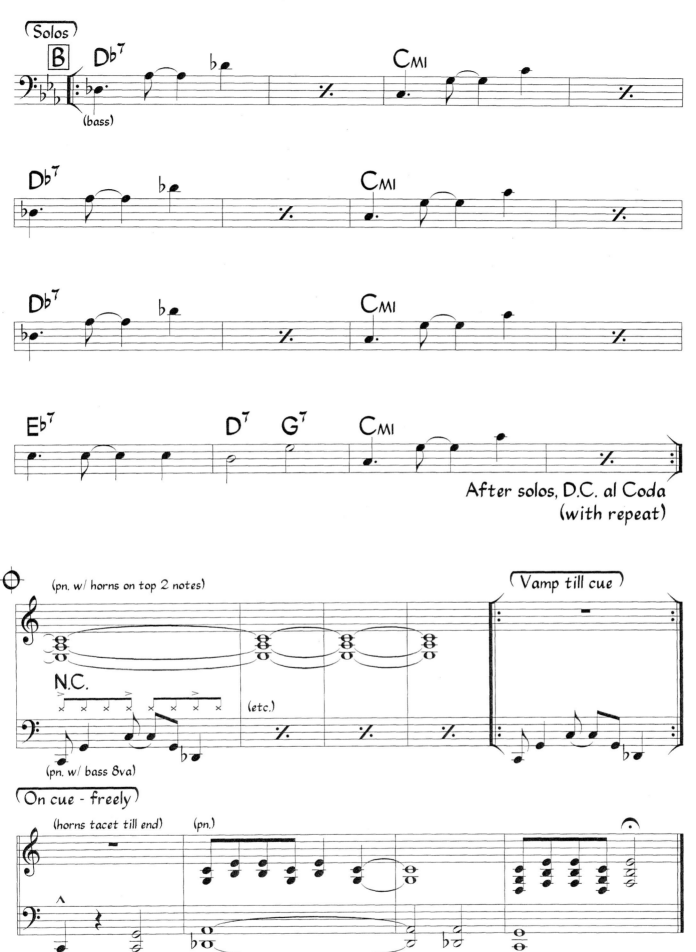

Too Marvelous For Words
(from "Ready, Willing And Able")

Music by Richard A. Whiting
Lyric by Johnny Mercer

so I'm bor - row - ing a love song from the birds, To

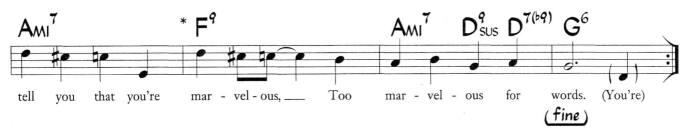

tell you that you're mar - vel - ous, ___ Too mar - vel - ous for words. (You're)

(fine)

Solo on ABC
After solos, D.S. al fine

* Originally

mar - vel - ous, Too

484

Too Much Saké

Horace Silver

(Solos) (Drums play Latin beat)

(bass)

* On the Db^{13}_{sus}/C chord, only the bass plays the C bass note.

Trouble Is A Man

Alec Wilder

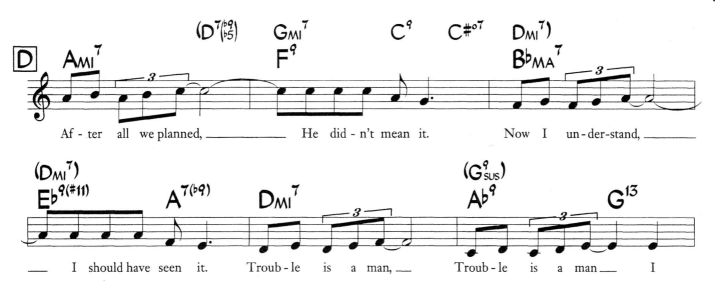

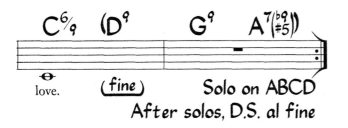

love. (fine) Solo on ABCD
After solos, D.S. al fine

Originally written 1 step higher, in D.

Twilight World

Music by Marian McPartland
Lyric by Johnny Mercer

Slow Bossa Nova

C
B♭MA7 B♭MI7 E♭9SUS E♭7(♭9) A♭MA7
twi - light world, don't let it slip a - way.
A♭MI7 D♭9SUS D♭7(♭9) G♭MA7 F7(#5) F7(♭9)/E♭ DMI7(♭5) G7(♭9)
Come take it while we may and let it be - gin. Let's find our
CMI7 F9SUS FMI7 F7(♭9) B♭(add 9)(GMI7 CMI7 F7)
twi - light world be - fore the night sets in.

Two For The Road

(Theme from "Two For The Road")

Music by Henry Mancini
Lyric by Leslie Bricusse

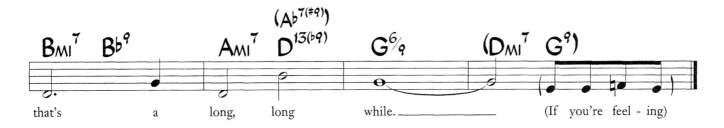

The Underdog

Music by Al Cohn
Lyric by Dave Frishberg

494

Mr. Frishberg prefers that the first chord of bar 3 of the introduction and also bar 3 of letter D be Gmi9 instead of Bbmi9.

Until It's Time For You To Go

Buffy Sainte-Marie

Roberta Flack performs this as a slow 12/8 ballad. The alternate changes are hers.

Until The Real Thing Comes Along

Mann Holinger, Alberta Nichols
Sammy Cahn, Saul Chaplin & L.E. Freeman

Solo on ABC
After solos,
D.S. al fine

Valdez In The Country

Music by Donny Hathaway
Lyric by Walter Lee & Frank Moss
(as played by George Benson)

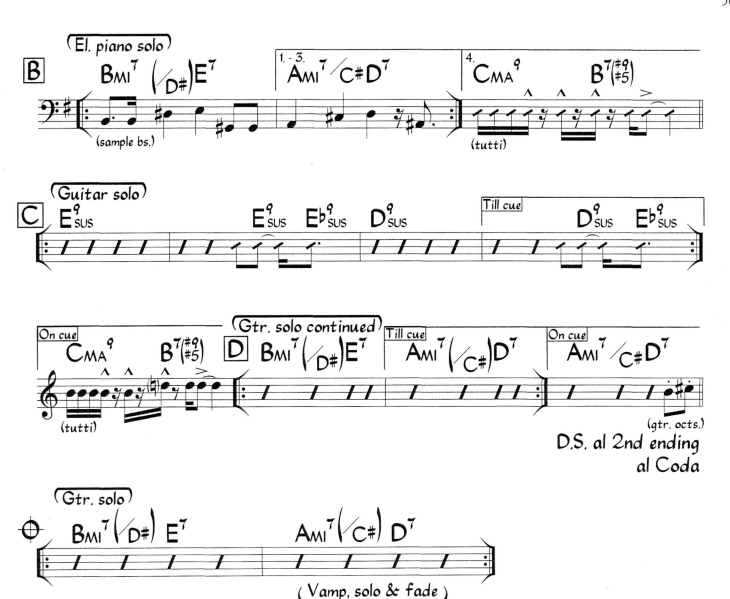

Walk On By

Music by Burt Bacharach
Lyric by Hal David

Wynton Kelly performed this Medium, straight ahead.

Photo by Jim Marshall

CHARLES MINGUS

Walkin'

Richard Carpenter
(As played by Miles Davis)

* In later versions Miles played this very fast and free.

We're In This Love Together

Roger Murrah
Keith Stegall

(As sung by Al Jarreau)

506

508

What A Fool Believes

Michael McDonald
Kenny Loggins
(As performed by the Doobie Brothers)

Chord progressions are more detailed in the rhythm part.

What A Fool Believes (Rhythm Section)

(sample bs.)

(bs. etc.)

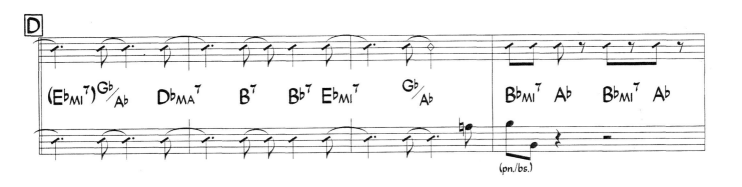

(pn./bs.)

(bs.)

V.S. (turn page)

Note: on main part B, C, D, & E are written as a repeat.

D.S., repeat letter E (omit 1st ending)
and fade out in letter E, 2nd x.

What Am I Here For?

515

SLAM STEWART

What Is This Thing Called Love?

(from "Wake Up And Dream")

Cole Porter

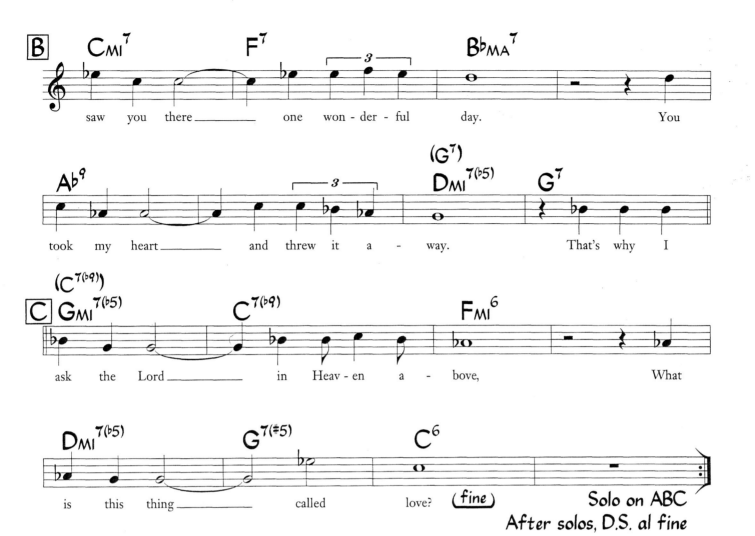

518

What The World Needs Now

Music by Burt Bacharach
Lyric by Hal David

What the world needs now is love, sweet love.
It's the on-ly thing___ that there's just___ too lit-tle of. What the
world needs now is love, sweet love.
No, not just for some, ___ but for ev-'ry-one. ___

Lord, we don't need an-oth-er moun-tain. There are
Lord, we don't need an-oth-er mead-ow. There are

moun-tains and hill-sides e-nough to climb. ___ There are
corn-fields and wheat-fields e-nough to grow. ___ There are

o-ceans and riv-ers e-nough to cross, E-nough to last
sun-beams and moon-beams e-nough to shine. Oh, lis-ten, Lord

till the end of time. ___ What the
if you want to know. ___

Solo on AB
After solos,
D.S. al Coda

(F#MI⁷)   B⁷(#5) G⁷(♭9))
B⁷   E⁷   C C⁶/₉

ev - 'ry - one.____   No, not just for some,____ Oh, but

Extended ending

BMI⁷   EMI⁷   A⁹   D⁹sus   G⁶/₉

just   for   ev - 'ry - one.____

Original ending

BMI⁷   CMA⁷   D⁷   G⁶

just   for   ev - 'ry - one.____

Letter B is originally written:

B EMI⁹

Lord, we don't need an - oth - er moun - tain.____ There are

DMI⁹   G⁹   CMA⁷   C⁶

moun - tains and hill - sides e - nough to climb.____ There are

DMI⁹   G⁹   CMA⁷   EMI⁷

o - ceans and riv - ers e - nough to cross,____ E - nough to last____

A⁷   D⁹sus

till the end of time.____ What the

Wheelers And Dealers

David Frishberg

The original lyric 2 bars before letter B (3rd verse) was "like unsatisfiable satyrs." It has been revised by the composer.
This chart is in Dave Frishberg's original key. Irene Kral sang this in D minor.

When A Man Loves A Woman

Calvin Lewis
Andrew Wright
(as performed by Percy Sledge)

D.S. for optional solos
Fade out last x

On Percy Sledge's original version the form is ABC (1st verse and chorus), AB (2nd verse), repeat A and fade out.
The written melody fits the first verse only.

When The World Was Young

Music by Philippe Block
Lyric by Johnny Mercer and Angele Vannier

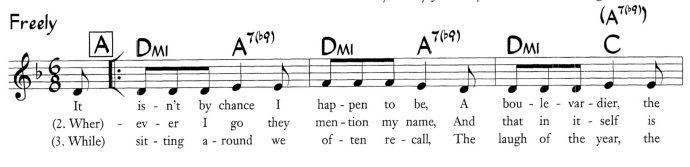

It is-n't by chance I hap-pen to be, A bou-le-var-dier, the
(2. Wher)-ev-er I go they men-tion my name, And that in it-self is
(3. While) sit-ting a-round we of-ten re-call, The laugh of the year, the

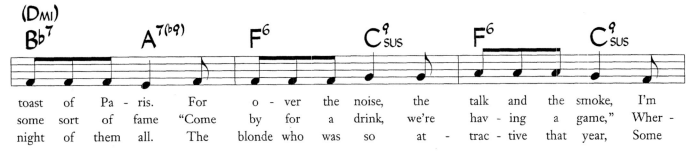

toast of Pa-ris. For o-ver the noise, the talk and the smoke, I'm
some sort of fame "Come by for a drink, we're hav-ing a game," Wher-
night of them all. The blonde who was so at-trac-tive that year, Some

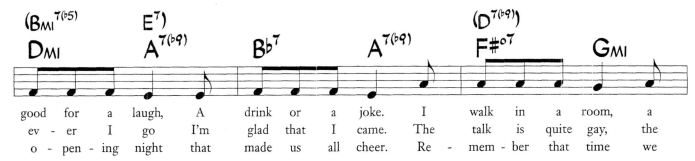

good for a laugh, A drink or a joke. I walk in a room, a
ev-er I go I'm glad that I came. The talk is quite gay, the
o-pen-ing night that made us all cheer. Re-mem-ber that time we

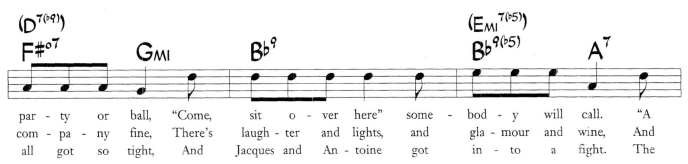

par-ty or ball, "Come, sit o-ver here" some-bod-y will call. "A
com-pa-ny fine, There's laugh-ter and lights, and gla-mour and wine, And
all got so tight, And Jacques and An-toine got in-to a fight. The

drink for M'-sieur! A drink for us all!" But how man-y times I stop and re-call.
beau-ti-ful girls and some of them mine. But oft-en my eyes see a dif-f'rent shine.
gen-darmes who came, passed out like a light, I laugh with the rest, It's all ver-y bright.

Medium Slow Waltz

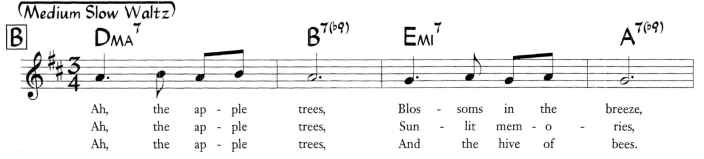

Ah, the ap-ple trees, Blos-soms in the breeze,
Ah, the ap-ple trees, Sun-lit mem-o-ries,
Ah, the ap-ple trees, And the hive of bees.

That we walked a - mong, Ly - ing in the hay,
Where the ham - mock swung, On our backs we'd lie,
Where we once got stung, Sum - mers at Bor - deaux,

Games we used to play, While the rounds were sung, On - ly yes - ter -
Look - ing at the sky Till the stars were strung, On - ly last Ju -
Row - ing the ba - teau, Where the wil - low hung, Just a dream a -

day, When the world was young. 2. Wher -
ly, When the world was young. 3. While
go, When the world was

young.

When Your Lover Has Gone

(from "Blond Crazy")

E.A. Swan

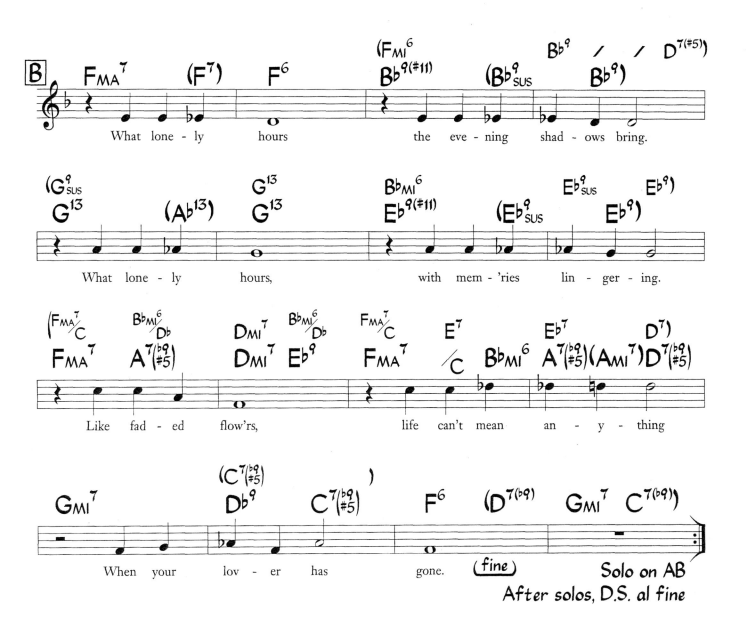

Primary chords in parentheses may be used for head only.
Originally in G, this tune is often played in A flat as well.

Where Or When

(from "Babes In Arms")

Music by Richard Rodgers
Lyric by Lorenz Hart

Solo on ABC
After solos, D.S. al fine

Who Cares?
(So Long As You Care For Me)

George Gershwin
Ira Gershwin

Long as you've _____ got a kiss that con - quers.
Long as your _____ kiss in - tox - i - cates me!

Why should I care? Life is
one long _____ ju - bi - lee, So long as
I care _____ for you _____ And
you care _____ for me. _____

Solo on AB
(fine) After solos, D.S. al fine

* Originally:

kiss that con - quers

* Cannonball Adderley played these 2 bars this way:

Why Try To Change Me Now?

Music by Cy Coleman
Lyric by Joseph McCarthy

534

laugh, ____ let them frown. You know I'll love you____ till the moon's ____ up-side down.

Don't ___ you re-mem-ber, ____ I was al - ways your clown. Why try to change me now?

Letter A, bars 1 & 9, are often played or sung:

With A Song In My Heart

(from "Spring Is Here")

Music by Richard Rodgers
Lyric by Lorenz Hart

He: Though I know that we meet ev-'ry night And we could-n't have changed since the last time, To my joy and de-light it's a new kind of love at first sight. Though it's you and it's I all the time Ev-'ry meet-ing's a mar-vel-ous pas-time, You're in-creas-ing-ly sweet, So when-ev-er we hap-pen to meet I greet you

She: Oh, the moon's not a moon for a night, And these stars will not twin-kle and fade out. And the words in my ears will re-sound for the rest of my years. In the morn-ing I'll find with de-light Not a note of our mu-sic is played out, It will be just as sweet, And an air that I'll live to re-peat:

With a song in my heart, I be-hold your a-dor-a-ble face, Just a song at the start, But it soon is a hymn to your grace.

536

* Also performed Double X (Medium or Fast), with each written bar equalling 2 bars.

You And The Night And The Music

(from "Revenge With Music")

Music by Arthur Schwartz
Lyric by Howard Dietz

* Also performed Bright or Latin (Ballad or Double Time).

You Are There

Music by Johnny Mandel
Lyric by Dave Frishberg

dis - tant star at dawn, my dear - est dream is gone, I of - ten think___ there's

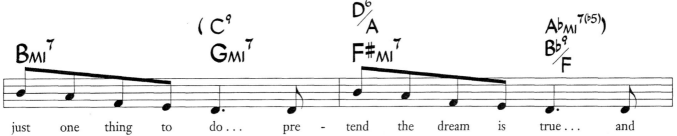

just one thing to do... pre - tend the dream is true... and

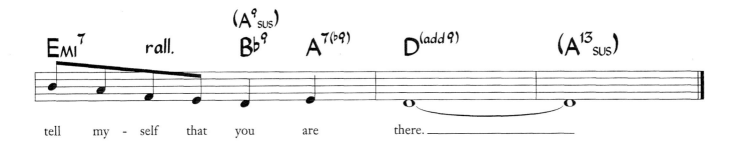

tell my - self that you are there._____

You Are Too Beautiful

(from "Hallelujah, I'm A Bum")

Music by Richard Rodgers
Lyric by Lorenz Hart

Solo on ABC
After solos, D.S. al fine

You Do Something To Me
(from "Fifty Million Frenchmen")

Cole Porter

Solo on ABC
After solos, D.S. al fine

You Go To My Head

Music by J. Fred Coots
Lyric by Haven Gillespie

You Make Me Feel Brand New

Thom Bell
Linda Creed
(as performed by the Stylistics)

You Make Me Feel So Young

(from "Three Little Girls In Blue")

Music by Josef Myrow
Lyric by Mack Gordon

You Taught My Heart To Sing

Music by McCoy Tyner
Lyric by Sammy Cahn
(As performed by Dianne Reeves)

Ballad

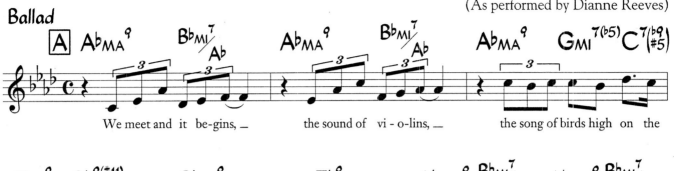

We meet and it be-gins, __ the sound of vi-o-lins, __ the song of birds high on the

wing. You taught my heart to sing.

Why does this heart of mine __ feel like a Val-en-tine? __ You smile and sud-den-ly it's

spring. You taught my heart to sing.

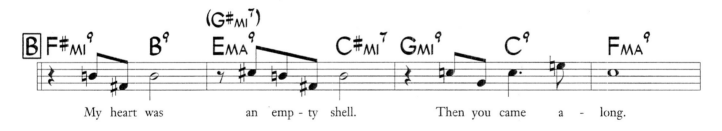

My heart was an emp-ty shell. Then you came a - long.

Now my heart's a car-o-sel filled __ with song.

The mir-a-cle of you __ will last my whole life through. __ You're all I'll keep re-mem-ber-

ing. You taught my heart to sing.

Solo on ABC
After solos, D.C. al Coda

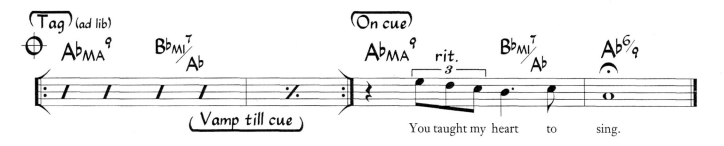

(Vamp till cue)

You taught my heart to sing.

McCoy Tyner's version
Medium (Freely)

(etc.)

Diane Reeves sings this in E flat. The original key is A flat.

552

You Took Advantage Of Me

(from "Present Arms")

Music by Richard Rodgers
Lyric by Lorenz Hart

Solo on ABC
After solos, D.S. al fine

You'd Be So Nice To Come Home To

(from "Something To Shout About")

Cole Porter

Solo on ABCD
after solos, D.S. al fine

You'll Never Know

Music by Harry Warren
Lyric by Mack Gordon

went with you. I speak your name in my ev-

'ry prayer. If there is some oth-er way to

prove that I love you, I swear I don't know how.

You'll nev-er know if you don't know now.

(fine)   Solo on AB
After solos, D.S. al fine

You're The Top
(from "Anything Goes")

Cole Porter

560

Ben - del bon - net, A Shake-speare son - net, You're Mick-y Mouse. __

You're the Nile,   You're the Tow'r of Pi - sa,

you're the smile   on the Mo - na Li - sa;

I'm a worth-less check, __ a to - tal wreck, __ a flop,   But if,

ba - by, I'm __ the bot-tom, You're __ the top!   (fine)   Solo on ABCD
                                                              After solos, D.S. al fine

ADDITIONAL REFRAINS:

You're the top! You're Mahatma Gandhi.
You're the top! You're Napoleon brandy.
You're the purple light of a summer night in Spain.
You're the National Gall'ry,
You're Garbo's sal'ry, You're cellophane.
You're sublime, You're a turkey dinner,
You're the time of the Derby winner.
I'm a toy balloon that's fated soon to pop,
But if, baby, I'm the bottom,
You're the top!

You're the top! You're a Ritz hot toddy.
You're the top! You're a Brewster body.
You're the boats that glide on a sleepy Zuider Zee.
You're a Nathan panning,
You're Bishop Manning, You're broccoli.
You're a prize, You're a night at Coney,
You're the eyes of Irene Bordoni.
I'm a broken doll, a fol-de-rol, a blop,
But if, baby, I'm the bottom,
You're the top!

You're the top! You're an Arrow collar.
You're the top! You're a Coolidge dollar.
You're the nimble tread of the feet of Fred Astaire,
You're an O'Neill drama,
You're Whistler's mama, You're Camembert.
You're a rose, You're Inferno's Dante,
You're the nose on the great Durante,
I'm just in the way, as the French would "De trop,"
But if, baby, I'm the bottom,
You're the top!

You're the top! You're a Waldorf salad.
You're the top! You're a Berlin ballad.
You're a baby grand of a lady and a gent.
You're an old Dutch master,
You're Mrs. Astor, You're Pepsodent.
You're romance, You're the steppes of Russia,
You're the pants on a Roxy usher.
I'm a lazy lout that's just about to stop,
But if, baby, I'm the bottom,
You're the top!

You're the top! You're a dance in Bali.
You're the top! You're a hot tamale.
You're an angel, you, simply too, too, too diveen.
You're a Botticelli,
You're Keats, you're Shelley, You're Ovaltine.
You're a boon, You're the dam at Boulder,
You're the moon over Mae West's shoulder.
I'm a nominee of the G.O.P. or GOP,
But if, baby, I'm the bottom,
You're the top!

You're the top! You're the Tower of Babel.
You're the top! You're the Whitney Stable.
By the river Rhine, You're a sturdy stein of beer,
You're a dress from Saks's,
You're next years taxes, You're stratosphere.
You're my thoist, You're a Drumstick Lipstick,
You're de foist in da Irish Svipstick.
I'm a frightened frog that can find no log to hop,
But if, baby, I'm the bottom,
You're the top!

Yours Is My Heart Alone

Music by Franz Lehar
Original Lyric by Ludwig Herzer & Fritz Lohner
English Lyric by Harry B. Smith

Jazz versions differ greatly from the original concept of this song.
Originally written in the key of C.

BILL EVANS

Appendix I - Sample Drum Parts

Transcribed by Kendrick Freeman, San Francisco Bay Area drummer and percussionist.

EXPLANATION OF NOTATION

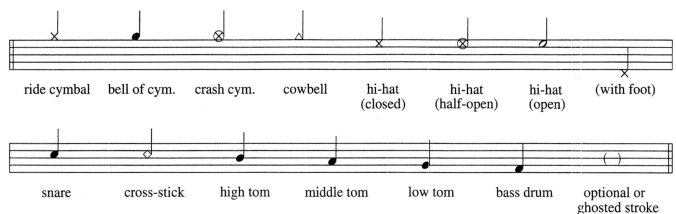

ride cymbal   bell of cym.   crash cym.   cowbell   hi-hat (closed)   hi-hat (half-open)   hi-hat (open)   (with foot)

snare   cross-stick   high tom   middle tom   low tom   bass drum   optional or ghosted stroke

CAUGHT UP IN THE RAPTURE

I WILL BE HERE FOR YOU

(bass drum varies with bass)

LOVE SPEAKS LOUDER THAN WORDS

(16th feel)

MINUTE BY MINUTE

(Intro)

MINUTE BY MINUTE (Continued)

PEOPLE MAKE THE WORLD GO 'ROUND

PIANO IN THE DARK

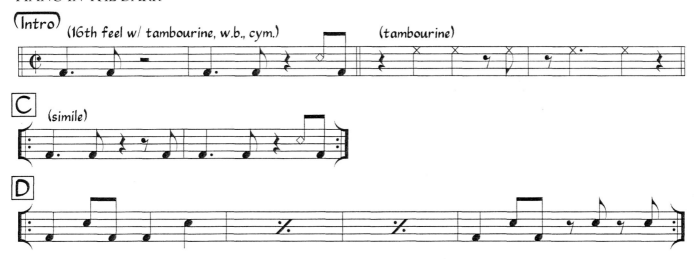

PICK UP THE PIECES

(drums catch horn figures)

REAL LOVE

SOMETHING TO TALK ABOUT

SOUL MAN

SUITE: JUDY BLUE EYES

TAKIN' IT TO THE STREET

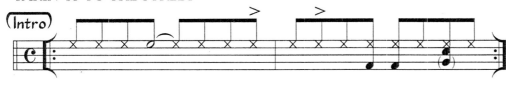

WHAT A FOOL BELIEVES

YOU MAKE ME FEEL BRAND NEW

After You - Published sheet music. Bobbe Norris' "CloseUp", Helen Merrill's "I Get A Kick Out Of You - The Cole Porter Songbook, Volume 2", "Kenny Drew Jr. at Maybeck"

Again - Published sheet music. Mark Murphy's "Stolen Moments", "Etta James Sings For Lovers", "Dinah Washington and Brook Benton - The Two Of Us"

Agua De Beber - Published sheet music. Ella Fitzgerald's "Ella á Nice", "The Wonderful World Of Antonio Carlos Jobim", "The Astrud Gilberto Album"

Ain't No Sunshine - "Bill Withers' Greatest Hits", Grover Washington, Jr.'s "Inner City Blues"

Alice In Wonderland - Bill Evans' "Sunday At The Village Vanguard", Bill Evans' "The Secret Sessions", Tom Lellis' "Taken To Heart"

All About Ronnie - Published sheet music. Chris Conners' "Lover Come Back To Me", Dominique Eade's "When The Wind Was Cool"

All My Tomorrows - Published sheet music. Mark Murphy's "What A Way To Go", "The Concord All-Stars On Cape Cod", Nancy Wilson's "Yesterday's Love Songs, Today's Blues", Shirley Horn's "You Won't Forget Me"

All Of You - Published sheet music. Ella Fitzgerald's "The Cole Porter Songbook, Volume 1", Miles Davis' "My Funny Valentine", Helen Merrill's "I Get A Kick Out Of You - The Cole Porter Songbook, Volume 2", Sonny Clark's "Blues In The Night", The Modern Jazz Quartet's "Concorde", "Annie Ross Sings Songs With Gerry Mulligan"

All Of You (Bill Evans' version) - Bill Evans' "Sunday At The Village Vanguard"

All The Way - Published sheet music. Charlie Haden, Billy Higgins & Enrico Pieranunzi's "First Song", Woody Shaw's "Setting Standards", Patrick Williams' "Sinatraland", Frank Sinatra's "My Way", "The Ralph Sharon Trio Swings The Sammy Cahn Songbook", Lena Horne from the compilation "It's Magic: Capitol Sings Sammy Cahn"

All Through The Night - Published sheet music. Paul Desmond's "Easy Living", Charlie Haden & Quartet West's "Now Is The Time", Ella Fitzgerald's "The Cole Porter Songbook, Volume 1", "Dick Hyman Plays The Great American Songbook", "The Phil Woods Quartet At The Vanguard"

Alone Together - Published sheet music. Paul Desmond's "Take Ten", Aki and Joe Henderson's "Humpty Dumpty", Dave McKenna's "Dancing In The Dark", Kenny Dorham's "Quiet Kenny", "Chet Baker In Paris, Volume 2", Lee Konitz, Brad Mehldau and Charlie Haden's "Alone Together", Hank Jones, Ray Brown & Jimmie Smith's "Rockin' In Rhythm", Rob McConnell & The Boss Brass' "Overtime"

Am I Blue? - Published sheet music. Jackie & Roy's "High Standards", Joe Pass/Herb Ellis's "Two For The Road"

And The Angels Sing - Published sheet music. Ella Fitzgerald's "Lady Time", Benny Goodman's "Pure Gold", Jimmy Witherspoon's "Some Of My Best Friends Are The Blues"

Anything Goes - Published sheet music. "Sonny Criss Plays Cole Porter", Ella Fitzgerald's "The Cole Porter Songbook, Volume 1", "Frank Sinatra Sings The Select Cole Porter", Tony Bennett's "Basie Swings, Bennett Sings", Tal Farlow's "Anything Goes: The Cole Porter Songbook", "Adam Makowicz and George Mraz Live At Maybeck", "A Tribute To Oscar Peterson - Live At Town Hall"

As Time Goes By - Published sheet music. Mark Murphy's "Bridging A Gap", Dexter Gordon's "Nights At The Keystone, Volume 3"

As We Speak - Dave Sanborn's "As We Speak"

At Last - Published sheet music. Etta James from the compilation "Pleasantville Soundtrack", "Miles Davis And The Lighthouse All-Stars - At Last", Bob Grabeau from the compilation "Capitol Sings Harry Warren - An Affair To Remember"

At Long Last Love - Published sheet music. Ella Fitzgerald's "Dream Dancing", "Frank Sinatra Sings The Select Cole Porter", Bill Henderson's "Night And Day - The Cole Porter Songbook", Grant Green's "I Want To Hold Your Hand"

Autumn Nocturne - Published sheet music. "The Standard Sonny Rollins", "The Mark Murphy Songbook", Bruce Foreman's "Foreman On The Job", Cassandra Wilson's "Blue Skies"

Bags' Groove - The Modern Jazz Quartet's "Blues At Carnegie Hall", "Modern Jazz Quartet - MJQ 40", Milt Jackson's "Big Mouth", The Modern Jazz Quartet's "MJQ And Friends", Hank Jones, Ray Brown & Jimmie Smith's "Rockin' In Rhythm", "A Tribute To Oscar Peterson - Live At Town Hall"

Baltimore Oriole - Published sheet music. Mark Murphy's "Song For The Geese", Bob Dorough's "Yardbird Suite (aka Devil May Care)", Carmen McRae's "American Popular Song"

A Beautiful Friendship - Published sheet music. "Joe Williams Live", Shirley Horn's "Close Enough For Love", "Nat King Cole Shows, Volume 1", James Williams and ICU's "We've Got What You Need", "Scott Hamilton Plays Ballads", Marlena Shaw's "Dangerous", Jean Ronne's "Daydream"

Begin The Beguine - Published sheet music. Art Tatum's "Solo Masterpieces, Volume 3", Ella Fitzgerald's "The Cole Porter Songbook, Volume 1", Gordon MacRae's "In Concert", Charlie Parker's "The Cole Porter Songbook", "Dick Hyman Plays The Great American Songbook"

Bess, You Is My Woman - Published sheet music. Miles Davis' "Porgy And Bess", Joe Henderson's "Porgy And Bess", Dave Grusin's "The Gershwin Connection", George Cables' "By George", Bill Potts' "The Jazz Soul Of Porgy And Bess", "Buddy DeFranco and Oscar Peterson Play George Gershwin", Roland Hanna's "Essential Jazz Ballads"

The Best Is Yet To Come - Published sheet music. "Mel Torme And Friends", Nancy Wilson's "Yesterday's Love Songs, Today's Blues", Diane Schur's "In Tribute", Frank Sinatra's "It Might As Well Be Spring", "Great Ladies Of Song: Spotlight On Peggy Lee"

Bewitched - Published sheet music. "Frank Sinatra Sings The Select Rodgers & Hart", Ella Fitzgerald's "The Rodgers & Hart Songbook, Volume 2", Benny Carter & Oscar Peterson's "Alone Together", Paul Desmond's "Polkadots And Moonbeams", Ralph Moore's "Round Trip", The Concord All-Stars On Cape Cod", Toni Harper from the compilation "Sultry Ladies of Jazz", "New York Swing Tributes Rodgers & Hart", Nancy Wilson's "Yesterday's Love Songs, Today's Blues"

Bidin' My Time - Published sheet music. Jackie & Roy's "High Standards", Sarah Vaughan's "The George Gershwin Songbook, Volume 2", "Ella Fitzgerald Sings The George And Ira Gershwin Songbook", Johnny Hartman's "Gershwin Standard Time", Nate King Cole from the compilation "Rhapsody In Blue: Blue Note Plays The Music Of George And Ira Gershwin"

Blackberry Winter - Published sheet music. Marlena Shaw's "Dangerous", Lynda Jamison's "Know What I've Learned"

Blue And Sentimental - Published sheet music. "The Gene Ammons Story", Arnett Cobb's "Live At Sandy's", Michel Legrand's "Legrand Jazz", "John Colianni At Maybeck"

Blue Gardenia - Published sheet music. Bobbe Norris's "CloseUp", "Lee Morgan - Standards", "Dinah Washington Sings The Blues", Ahmad Jamal's "Chicago Revisited", Gloria Lynne's "Intimate Moments"

Blue Room - Published sheet music. "Miles Davis & Horns", Ella Fitzgerald's "The Rodgers And Hart Songbook, Volume 1", Gene Ammons' "Angel Eyes", "The Red Garland Trio", Hank Jones "Urbanity", "Sonny Rollins", Bing Crosby's "Bing Sings Whilst Bregman Swings"

Blues In The Night - Published sheet music. Art Pepper's "The Art Of The Ballad", Ella Fitzgerald's "American Popular Song", "Kenny Drew Plays The Music Of Harry Warren And Harold Arlen", Sonny Clark's "Blues In The Night", "Louis Armstrong Meets Oscar Peterson"

Bluesette - Published sheet music. Toots Thielemans' "Slow Motion", "Toots Thielemans - The Silver Collection", Cleo Laine's "Jazz", Morgana King's "Taste Of Honey", Ray Charles' "My Kind Of Jazz"

Born To Be Blue. - Published sheet music. Wynton Kelly's "Full View", Clifford Brown from the compilation "Verve Jazz 'Round Midnight", Ike Quebec from "The Complete Blue Note Recordings of Grant Green/Sonny Clark", Eddie Harris' "The In Sound/Mean Greens", "An Evening With George Shearing & Mel Torme", "Mel Torme: Compact Jazz"

But Not For Me - Published sheet music. Sarah Vaughan's "The George Gershwin Songbook, Volume 2", "Anita O'Day At Mister Kelly's", "Ella Fitzgerald Sings The George And Ira Gershwin Songbook", Dinah Washington's " 'S Wonderful: The Gershwin Songbook", Miles Davis' "Bag's Groove"

But Not For Me (Coltrane's version) - John Coltrane's "My Favorite Things"

Caught Up In The Rapture - Published sheet music. Anita Baker's "Rapture"

Charade - Published sheet music. "Sarah Vaughan Sings The Mancini Songbook", Henry Mancini's "Charade", James Moody's "Moody Plays Mancini" "Monica Mancini", Andy Williams' "The Music Of Henry Mancini", Jim Ferguson's "Not Just A Pretty Bass", Royce Campbell's "Tribute Mancini"

The Christmas Waltz - Published sheet music. Dianne Reeves' "More Mistletoe Magic", "An Oscar Peterson Christmas", Dave McKenna's "Christmas Ivory"

Close Enough For Love - Published sheet music. Stan Getz' "The Dolphin", "Sue Raney Sings The Music Of Johnny Mandel", Jacky Terrasson's "Lover Man", Shirley Horn's "Close Enough For Love", Bobbi Rogers & Gene Bertoncini's "Crystal And Velvet"

Close To You - Published sheet music. Ella Fitzgerald's "Ella á Nice", Joey D'Francesco's "All Of Me", Dionne Warwick's "I Say A Little Prayer For You"

Come Fly With Me - Published sheet music. "Frank Sinatra - A Man And His Music", Monty Alexander's "Memories Of Jilly", Birelli Langrene's "Blue Eyes"

The Continental - Published sheet music. "Cal Tjader's Latin Concert", J.J. Johnson and Kai Winding's "Jay And Kai + Six", Django Reinhardt's "Un Géant Sur Son Nuage, Volume 3"

Cotton Tail - Published big band arrangement. Duke Ellington's "Fargo, ND, November 7, 1940", "Duke Ellington: The Blanton-Webster Band", "Ella Fitzgerald Sings The Duke Ellington Songbook", Wes Montgomery's "So Much Guitar", Duke Ellington and Billie Strayhorn's "Great Times!", Andre Previn's "After Hours", "Kenny Clarke Meets The Detroit Jazzmen"

Crazy He Calls Me - Published sheet music. "Jimmy Guiffre With Jim Hall", Peggy Stern's "Room Enough", Randy Johnson's "Walk On", Ahmad Jamal's "Poinciana"

Crazy Rhythm - Published sheet music. "Stan Getz And J.J. Johnson At The Opera House", Coleman Hawkins and Lester Young's "Classic Tenors", Red Garland's "Dig It!", Bud Powell's "The Complete Verve Recordings"

Cute - Published sheet music. "The World Of Count Basie", Count Basie's "Montreux '77", Count Basie's "The Atomic Band Live In Europe", "Stanley Turrentine/Shirley Scott: Priceless Jazz Collection"

Dancing In The Dark - Published sheet music. Fred Hersch's "Dancing In The Dark", Joe Pass' "Blues For Fred", Sonny Clark's "Blues In The Night", Dave McKenna's "Dancing In The Dark"

Dancing On The Ceiling - Published sheet music. "Frank Sinatra Sings The Select Rodgers & Hart", Ella Fitzgerald's "The Rodgers & Hart Songbook, Volume 1", Hank Jones, Ray Brown & Jimmie Smith's "Rockin' In Rhythm", "Chet Baker Sings: It Could Happen To You"

Day In, Day Out - Published sheet music. Jimmy Smith's "I'm Movin' On", "Ella Fitzgerald Sings The Johnny Mercer Songbook", "Horace Silver Trio", "Dream: Johnny Costa Plays Johnny Mercer"

Days Of Wine And Roses - Published sheet music. "Keith Jarrett At The Blue Note", Henry Mancini's "The Days Of Wine And Roses", "The Tony Bennett/Bill Evans Album", Cyrus Chestnut's "Nut", Dave Grusin's "Two For The Road", Bobbe Norris' "The Beginning", "Sarah Vaughan Sings The Mancini Songbook", "Monica Mancini", Patti Page's "The Music Of Henry Mancini", "An Evening With Herb Ellis", Milt Jackson's "Big Mouth"

Dedicated To You - Published sheet music. "John Coltrane And Johnny Hartman"

Deep Purple - Published sheet music. "Suddenly It's The Hi-Los", Art Tatum's "The Complete Pablo Solo Recordings", "The Divine Sarah Vaughan", "Great Ladies Of Song: Spotlight On Peggy Lee", "Stanley Turrentine/Shirley Scott: Priceless Jazz Collection"

The Dock Of The Bay - Published sheet music. "Otis Redding's Greatest Hits"

Don't Be Blue - Michael Franks' "Sleeping Gypsy", Mark Murphy's "Stolen Moments"

Don't Worry 'Bout Me - Published sheet music. "The Essential Billie Holiday", Frank Sinatra's "This Is Sinatra!", Gloria Lynne's "Golden Classics", Red Garland's "The Nearness Of You"

Doodlin' - Published sheet music. "Horace Silver And The Jazz Messengers", Dee Dee Bridgewater's "Love And Peace"

Doxy - Sonny Rollins' "Tenor Titan", Dexter Gordon's "Both Sides Of Midnight", "The Fred Hersch Trio Plays. . . "

Dream Dancing - Published sheet music. Zoot Sims' "Warm Tenor", Ella Fitzgerald's "Dream Dancing", Meredith D'Ambrosio's "South To A Warmer Place", Mary Stallings' "Fine And Mellow", Rob McConnell, Ed Bickert & Don Thompson's "Three For The Road"

Dreamsville - Published sheet music. Dave Grusin's "Two For The Road", Henry Mancini's "Music From 'Peter Gunn' ", Rob McConnell, Ed Bickert & Don Thompson's "Three For The Road", Lola Albright's "The Music Of Henry Mancini"

Easy To Love - Published sheet music. "Charlie Parker Plays Standards", "Sonny Criss Plays Cole Porter", Charlie Parker's "The Cole Porter Songbook", "Dick Hyman Plays The Great American Songbook", Sonny Stitt's " Anything Goes: The Cole Porter Songbook", "Oscar Peterson Plays The Cole Porter Songbook", Billie Holiday's "Night And Day: The Cole Porter Songbook", Gene Ammons' "Jug"

Embraceable You - Published sheet music. Joe Williams' "In Good Company", "Ella Fitzgerald Sings The George And Ira Gershwin Songbook", Billie Holiday's "Body And Soul", "Clifford Brown And Strings", Herbie Hancock's "Gershwin's World", Sarah Vaughan's "The George Gershwin Songbook, Volume 2", "Bill Evans At The Montreux Jazz Festival", Andre Previn's "We Got Rhythm - A Gershwin Songbook", "Charlie Parker Plays Standards", Chet Baker's "Embraceable You", Frank Rosolino from the compilation "Rhapsody In Blue: Blue Note Plays The Music Of George And Ira Gershwin", Jack Jones' "The Gershwin Album"

Everything Must Change - Published sheet music. Quincy Jones' "The Dude", George Benson's "In Flight"

Falling In Love With Love - Published sheet music. Keith Jarrett's "Standards Live", Ron McClure's "Tonight Only", Oscar Peterson's "The London Concert Royal Festival Hall, 1978", "Kenny Dorham And Friends", Grant Green's "Reaching Out", Dinah Shore from the compilation "Isn't It Romantic - Capitol Sings Rodgers And Hart", Ahmad Jamal's "Cross Country Tour: 1958-1961", "New York Swing Tributes Rodgers And Hart", "Cannonball Adderley And Strings/Jump For Joy"

Fascinating Rhythm - Published sheet music. "Ella Fitzgerald Sings The George And Ira Gershwin Songbook", Sarah Vaughan's "The George Gershwin Songbook, Volume 2", Oscar Peterson's "The Song Is You", Antonio Carlos Jobim's "Passarim", "The Amazing Artistry Of Louis Bellson",

Matt Catingub's "George Gershwin 100", Dave Grusin's "The Gershwin Collection", Fred Astaire's " 'S Wonderful: The Gershwin Songbook"

A Felicidade - Published sheet music. "João Gilberto Interpreta Tom Jobim", "The Wonderful World Of Antonio Carlos Jobim", Joe Henderson's "Double Rainbow", Rosa Passos' "Curare", Monica Salmaso's "Antonio Carlos Jobim Songbook, Volume 3", Hendrik Meurkins' "Poema Brasileiro"

A Foggy Day - Published sheet music. Oscar Peterson's "The Song Is You", Dinah Washington's " 'S Wonderful: The Gershwin Songbook", "Ella Fitzgerald Sings The George And Ira Gershwin Songbook", Sarah Vaughan's "The George Gershwin Songbook, Volume 2", Wynton Marsalis' "Standards, Volume 1", "The Artistry Of Art Pepper", Chris Conner's "Lover Come Back To Me", Matt Catingub's "George Gershwin 100"

Forest Flower - Charles Lloyd's "Forest Flower" and "Soundtrack", "Charles Lloyd At His Best"

From This Moment On - Published sheet music. "Frank Sinatra Sings The Select Cole Porter", Ella Fitzgerald's "The Cole Porter Songbook, Volume 2", Anita O'Day's "I Get A Kick Out Of You: The Cole Porter Songbook, Volume 2", Johnny Griffin & Eddie "Lockjaw" Davis' "Tough Tenor Favorites", "Cy Coleman Trio"

Get Here - Published sheet music. "Brenda Russell: Greatest Hits", "The Very Best Of Oleta Adams"

Get Out Of Town - Published sheet music. Gerry Mulligan's "Jeru", Ella Fitzgerald's "The Cole Porter Songbook, Volume 2", "Cy Coleman Trio", Coleman Hawkins' "On Broadway"

The Girl From Ipanema - Published sheet music. Stan Getz & João Gilberto's "Getz/Gilberto", "Rosa Passos Canta Antonio Carlos Jobim", Rosa Passos' "Songbook: Antonio Carlos Jobim, 4", Ella Fitzgerald's "Pure Ella" and "Ella á Nice"

Give Me The Simple Life - Published sheet music. "An Evening With With George Shearing & Mel Torme", Ella Fitzgerald's "Ella Returns To Berlin", "Oscar Peterson Tracks", Donald Brown's "Piano Short Stories".

Good Bait - Published sheet music. John Coltrane's "Soultrane", Fats Navarro & Tadd Dameron's "Royal Roost Sessions 1948", "Milt Jackson's "Bebop", "Dameronia - Live At The Theatre Boulogne - Billancourt/Paris"

The Good Life - Published sheet music. "Ahmad Jamal Live At Bubba's", Oscar Peterson's "The Good Life", Frank Sinatra & Count Basie's "It Might As Well Be Swing", Carmen McRae's "Ms. Jazz"

Have You Met Miss Jones? - Published sheet music. McCoy Tyner's "Reaching Forth", Vincent Herring's "Secret Love", Ella Fitzgerald's "The Rodgers and Hart Songbook, Volume 1", "Smokin' With The Chet Baker Quintet", Louis Armstrong's "Louis Under The Stars", Frank Sinatra's "My Kind Of Broadway", "Bobby Short Celebrates Rodgers And Hart", Sarah Vaughan from the compilation "Isn't It Romantic - Capitol Sings Rodgers And Hart", "New York Swing Tributes Rodgers And Hart"

He Was Too Good To Me - Published sheet music. Chet Baker's "She Was Too Good To Me", Meredith D'Ambrosio's "South To A Warmer Place"

Hello - Published sheet music. Lionel Richie's "Can't Slow Down", Luther Vandross' "Songs"

Hey There - Published sheet music. Bill Evans' "Conversations With Myself", Hal Galper's "Invitation To A Concert", Grant Green's "The Latin Bit"

Hot House - "Charlie Parker At St. Nick's", "Barry Harris Plays Tadd Dameron", Charlie Parker's "An Evening At Home With The Bird", "Dameronia - Live At The Theatre Boulogne-Billancourt/Paris", Warren Rand's "Dameron II-V"

A House Is Not A Home - Published sheet music. Stan Getz' "What The World Needs Now", McCoy Tyner's "What The World Needs Now"

How Do You Keep The Music Playing? - Published sheet music. George Benson's "Big Band Jazz", James Ingram's "Greatest Hits - The Power Of Great Music"

How Insensitive - Published sheet music. Antonio Carlos Jobim's "Antonio Brasileiro", "Rosa Passos Canta An Carlos Jobim", Bobbe Norris' "The Beginning", Nana Caymmi's "Brasil MPB"

How Little We Know - Published sheet music. Carmen McRae's "Here To Stay", Frank Sinatra's "The Capitol Years"

How Long Has This Been Going On? - Published sheet music. "Ella Fitzgerald Sings The George And Gershwin Songbook", Sarah Vaughan's "The George Gershwin Songbook, Volume 2", Dave Grusin's "The Gershwin Collection", "The Genius Of Coleman Hawkins", Ella Fitzgerald's " 'S Wonderful: The Gershwin Songbook", Herbie Hancock from the compilation "Round Midnight-Original Motion Picture Soundtrack", "Chet Baker Sings: It Could Happen To You", "Louis Armstrong Meets Oscar Peterson", Matt Catingub's "George Gershwin 100", Jack Jones' "The Gershwin Album", Suzannah McCorkle's "Someone To Watch Over Me"

I Can't Get Started - Published sheet music. "Piano Bar by Erroll Garner", "Cannonball Adderley/Nancy Wilson", Erroll Garner's "Body And Soul", Morgana King's "Stardust", "Buck Clayton Meets Joe Turner", Charlie Parker's "Jazz At The Philharmonic-1946", Charles Mingus' "Jazz Portraits: Mingus In Wonderland"

I Concentrate On You - Published sheet music. Max Roach's "Anything Goes: The Cole Porter Songbook", "Frank Sinatra Sings The Select Cole Porter", Ella Fitzgerald's "The Cole Porter Songbook, Volume 2", "Francis Albert Sinatra And Antonio Carlos Jobim", Grant Green's "The Complete Quartets With Sonny Clark", Fred Astaire's "Night And Day: The Cole Porter Songbook"

I Could Write A Book - Published sheet music. Dinah Washington's "For Those In Love", Ella Fitzgerald's "The Rodgers And Hart Songbook, Volume 2", "Frank Sinatra Sings The Select Rodgers And Hart", Miles Davis' "Relaxin' ", Kenny Drew's "The Riverside Collection", Vic Damone from the compilation "Isn't It Romantic - Capitol Sings Rodgers And Hart"

I Cover The Waterfront - Published sheet music. George Shearing's "Jazz Concert", "Cannonball Adderley And Strings", Sonny Clark's "Blues In The Night", Hank Jones from Frank Morgan's "You Must Believe In Spring", "Charlie Parker At St. Nick's", "The Complete Capitol Recordings Of Art Tatum"

I Didn't Know About You - Published sheet music. Dinah Washington's "Our Love", Duke Ellington's "Black, Brown And Beige", Phil Woods and Jim McNeely's "Flowers For Hodges", Geoff Keezer's "Waiting In The Wings", Jo Stafford's "Jo + Jazz"

I Didn't Know What Time It Was - Published sheet music. Stan Getz' "Voices", Ella Fitzgerald's "The Rodgers And Hart Songbook, Volume 2", "Frank Sinatra Sings The Select Rodgers And Hart", "Charlie Parker At St. Nick's", Benny Carter's "Frenesi", Cassandra Wilson's "Blue Skies", "An Evening With Anita O'Day", Stephane Grappelli and McCoy Tyner's "One On One", "Bobby Short Celebrates Rodgers And Hart"

I Get A Kick Out Of You - Published sheet music. "Sonny Criss Plays Cole Porter", Dinah Washington's "The Cole Porter Songbook: Night And Day", Clifford Brown And Max Roach's "Anything Goes: The Cole Porter Songbook", "Frank Sinatra Sings The Select Cole Porter", Ella Fitzgerald's "The Cole Porter Songbook, Volume 1", Chris Conner from the compilation "Anything Goes: Capitol Sings Cole Porter", Louis Armstring's "I Get A Kick Out Of You: The Cole Porter Songbook, Volume 2", Benny Carter's "Frenesi", "Louis Armstrong Meets Oscar Peterson", Charlie Parker's "The Cole Porter Songbook", "The Piano Style Of Nat King Cole"

I Got Rhythm - Published sheet music. "Ella Fitzgerald Sings The George And Ira Gershwin Songbook", Sarah Vaughan's "The George Gershwin Songbook, Volume 2", Andre Previn's "We Got Rhythm - A Gershwin Songbook", Bill Evans and Bob Brookmeyer and also Frank Rosolino's version from the compilation "Rhapsody In Blue: Blue Note Plays The Music Of George And Ira Gershwin", Coleman Hawkins and Lester Young's "Classic Tenors", Charlie Parker's "Jazz At The Philharmonic-1946", Erroll Garner's "Magician/Gershwin And Kern", George Cables' "By George", "Django '35-'39 - The Quintet Of The Hot Club Of France", Matt Catingub's "George Gershwin 100", Suzannah McCorkle's "Someone To Watch Over Me"

Stephane Grappelli and McCoy Tyner's "One On One", "Buddy DeFranco And Oscar Peterson Play George Gershwin"

I Gotta Right To Sing The Blues - Published sheet music. Ella Fitzgerald's "The Harold Arlen Songbook, Volume 2", "The Essential Billie Holiday", "Eydie Gorme Swings The Blues", "Benny Goodman And His Orchestra 1931-1933"

I Guess I'll Have To Change My Plan - Published sheet music. Art Tatum from the compilation "Jazz Piano Anthology - Bop, Volume 2", "Mel Torme And Friends", Tony Bennett's "Steppin' Out", Frank Sinatra's "A Swingin' Affair"

I Had The Craziest Dream - Published sheet music. Kenny Dorham's "Quiet Kenny", George Shearing and Mel Torme's "An Elegant Evening", Lou Donaldson's "Play The Right Thing"

I Have The Feeling I've Been Here Before - Published sheet music. "The Very Best Of Carmen McRae", Carmen McRae's "Dream Of Life", Roger Kellaway and Red Mitchell's "Life's A Take"

I Love Paris - Published sheet music. Jackie Terrasson's "The Blue Note Years", "Frank Sinatra Sings The Select Cole Porter", "Ella Fitzgerald: The Cole Porter Songbook, Volume 2", "Cal Tjader's Latin Kick", Charlie Parker's "The Cole Porter Songbook", Jesse Davis' "Young At Art"

I Love You - Published sheet music. Bill Evans' "Montreux III", John Coltrane's "Lush Life", Oscar Peterson's "Anything Goes: The Cole Porter Songbook", Anita O'Day's "The Cole Porter Songbook - Night And Day", "Sonny Criss Plays Cole Porter", "Fond Memories Of Frank Rosolino", Milt Jackson's "Big Mouth", "An Evening With Herb Ellis"

I Loves You Porgy - Published sheet music. Bill Evans' "Waltz For Debby", "Bill Evans At The Montreux Jazz Festival", Miles Davis' "Porgy And Bess", Oscar Peterson's "Tristeza", Joe Henderson's "Porgy And Bess", Dave Grusin's "The Gershwin Collection", Nina Simone's " 'S Wonderful - The Gershwin Songbook", Fred Hersch's "Let Yourself Go: Live At Jordan Hall", Susannah McCorkle's "Someone To Watch Over Me", "Billie Holiday's Greatest Hits"

I May Be Wrong - Published sheet music. "Four Freshman And Five Saxes", Gerry Mulligan with Chubby Jackson's Orchestra's "Conception", Coleman Hawkins and Pee Wee Russell's "Jam Session In Swingsville"

I Only Have Eyes For You - Published sheet music. Oscar Peterson's "The Song Is You", Coleman Hawkins' "Verve Jazz Masters 34", Eddie "Lockjaw" Davis' "I Only Have Eyes For You", Andre Previn's "After Hours", Erroll Garner's "Magician/Gershwin And Kern", Dinah Shore from the compilation "An Affair To Remember: Capitol Sings Harry Warren", "The Sound Of The Flamingos", Morgana King's "Stardust", Joe Pass' "Song For Helen"

I Say A Little Prayer For You - Published sheet music. Dionne Warwick's "Dionne Sings Dionne", Aretha Franklin's "Aretha Now", Reuben Wilson's "Love Bug", "Wes Montgomery - Greatest Hits"

I Want To Be Happy - Published sheet music. "An Evening With Herb Ellis", Sonny Stitt/Bud Powell/J.J.Johnson's "I Want To Be Happy", Cliff Jackson's "Jam Session In Swingsville, featuring Coleman Hawkins And Pee Wee Russell", "Oscar Peterson Plays Vincent Youmans", "Art Farmer's "Live At The Half Note", Chick Corea's "Impressions"

I Was Doing All Right - Published sheet music. "Ella Fitzgerald Sings The George And Ira Gershwin Songbook", "Louis Armstrong Meets Oscar Peterson", Suzannah McCorkle's "Someone To Watch Over Me", Meredith D'Ambrosio's "Another Time"

I Will Be Here For You - Al Jarreau's "Jarreau"

I Will Wait For You - Published sheet music. Astrud Gilberto's "Look To The Rainbow", Oscar Peterson's "Exclusively For My Friends - The Lost Tapes"

I Wish I Knew - Published sheet music. Bill Evans' "Explorations", John Coltrane's "Ballads", Wes Montgomery's "While We're Young", Ahmad Jamal's "Ahmad's Blues", Stan Getz' "Pure Getz", Mary Stallings' "Manhattan Moods"

I Wish I Were In Love Again - Published sheet music. Tony Bennett's "More Great Rodgers And Hart Songs", Ella Fitzgerald's "The Rodgers And Hart Songbook, Volume 1", "Frank Sinatra Sings The Select Rodgers And Hart", "Bobby Short Celebrates Rodgers And Hart", Rosemary Clooney's "Show Tunes"

I'm A Fool To Want You - Published sheet music. Blue Mitchell's "Smooth As The Wind", "The Complete Dinah Washington On Mercury", Linda Ronstadt's "Lush Life", Paula West's "Restless"

I'm Gonna Laugh You Right Out Of My Life - Published sheet music. Milt Jackson's "In A New Setting", Natalie Cole's "Take A Look", Gloria Lynne's "Intimate Moments", Gary Bartz's "The Red And Orange Poems"

I've Got A Crush On You - Published sheet music. "Ella Fitzgerald Sings The George And Ira Gershwin Songbook", Sarah Vaughan's "The George Gershwin Songbook, Volume 1", "Zoot Sims And The Gershwin Brothers", Suzannah McCorkle's "Someone To Watch Over Me", Bill Henderson's " 'S Wonderful: The Gershwin Songbook", Matt Catingub's "George Gershwin 100", Jack Jones' "The Gershwin Album"

I've Got You Under My Skin - Published sheet music. Ella Fitzgerald's "Dream Dancing" and "The Cole Porter Songbook, Volume 2", "Frank Sinatra Sings The Select Cole Porter", Charlie Parker's "The Cole Porter Songbook", Dinah Washington's "Night And Day - The Cole Porter Songbook", Joe Henderson's "Tetragon", "Piano Bar By Erroll Garner", Bill Evans and Jim Hall's "Intermodulation", "Stan Getz Quartets", Chris Conner's "Lover Come Back To Me", Diana Krall's "When I Look In Your Eyes", Louis Prima and Kelly Smith from the compilation, "Anything Goes - Capitol Sings Cole Porter"

If There Is Someone Lovelier Than You - Published sheet music. Mark Levine's "One Notch Up", Enrico Pieranunzi's "New Lands", John Coltrane's "Settin' The Pace"

In The Days Of Our Love - Published sheet music. Marian McPartland's "At The Festival", Meredith D'Ambrosio's "The Cove", Peggy Lee's "Close Enough For Love"

In The Midnight Hour - Published sheet music. Wilson Pickett's "In The Midnight Hour"

Indian Summer - Published sheet music. "Stan Getz Quartets", Ron Carter and Jim Hall's "Telephone", Coleman Hawkins' "I Love You: Giants Of Jazz", Lee Konitz' "Conception".

Isn't It A Pity - Published sheet music. "Ella Fitzgerald Sings The George And Ira Gershwin Songbook", Sarah Vaughan's "The George Gershwin Songbook, Volume 2", Mel Torme's "Gershwin Standard Time", Shirley Horn's "Here's To Life", "Mel Torme And Friends", Steve Lawrence's "All About Love", Karen Akers' "Unchained Melody", Andre Previn's "We Got Rhythm - A Gershwin Songbook"

It Ain't Necessarily So - Published sheet music. Miles Davis' "Porgy And Bess", Joe Henderson's "Porgy And Bess", "Cal Tjader Plays Mambo", The Art Farmer/Benny Golson Jazztet's "Meet The Jazztet", "Buddy DeFranco And Oscar Peterson Play George Gershwin", Grant Green's "The Complete Quartets With Sonny Clark"

It Had To Be You - Published sheet music. Shirley Horn's "You Won't Forget Me", Jimmy McGriff's "Straight Up", Anita O'Day's "The Big Band Sessions", Lynda Jamison's "You And The Night And The Music", "Dinah Shore Sings, Andre Previn Plays"

It Never Entered My Mind - Published sheet music. Miles Davis' "Workin' ", "The Best Of Bud Powell On Verve", Stan Getz' "Cool Velvet", "The Essential Stan Getz: The Getz Songbook", Ella Fitzgerald's "The Rodgers And Hart Songbook, Volume 1", "Sarah Vaughan Sings The Rodgers And Hart Songbook", "Coleman Hawkins Encounters Ben Webster", "Frank Sinatra Sings The Select Rodgers And Hart", Linda Ronstadt's "Lush Life",

"Concord All-Stars On Cape Cod", "John Colianni At Maybeck"

It Was A Very Good Year - Published sheet music. James Moody's "Young At Heart", Eddie Harris' "The In Sound/Mean Greens", Wes Montgomery's "Goin' Out Of My Head", The Three Sounds from the compilation "Blue Note Plays Sinatra"

It's All Right With Me - Published sheet music. Erroll Garner's "Concerts By The Sea", "Frank Sinatra Sings The Select Cole Porter", "Ella Fitzgerald: The Cole Porter Songbook, Volume 2", Joe Gilman's "Treasure Chest", Cyrus Chestnut's "Nut", "Sonny Criss Plays Cole Porter", Dinah Shore's "Dinah Sings The Blues With Red"

It's De-Lovely - Published sheet music. Ella Fitzgerald's "The Cole Porter Songbook, Volume 2", Sarah Vaughan's "The Cole Porter Songbook - Night And Day"

It's Magic - Published sheet music. Carmen McRae's "Sarah - Dedicated To You", Dinah Washington's "What A Difference A Day Makes!", Eric Dolphy's "Far Cry", Keely Smith from the compilation "It's Magic - Capitol Sings Sammy Cahn", Abbey Lincoln's "It's Magic", "The Ralph Sharon Trio Swings The Sammy Cahn Songbook"

It's You Or No One - Published sheet music. McCoy Tyner's "Quartets", Bobbe Norris' "Out Of Nowhere", Ahmad Jamal's "Cross Country Tour: 1958-1961", "The Ralph Sharon Trio Swings The Sammy Cahn Songbook"

Johnny One Note - Published sheet music. Ella Fitzgerald's "The Rodgers And Hart Songbook, Volume 1", "Bobby Short Celebrates Rodgers And Hart"

Just One Of Those Things - Published sheet music. Charlie Parker's "The Cole Porter Songbook", "The Best Of Bud Powell On Verve", Coleman Hawkins' "Verve Jazz Masters 34", "The Piano Style Of Nat King Cole", "Louis Armstrong Meets Oscar Peterson", Ella Fitzgerald's "The Cole Porter Songbook, Volume 1", "Frank Sinatra Sings The Select Cole Porter", "Gil Evans Plus Ten", Bud Powell's "Anything Goes: The Cole Porter Songbook", "Sonny Criss Plays Cole Porter", Ella Fitzgerald's "Dream Dancing", Nat "King" Cole's "Just One Of Those Things", "Oscar Peterson Plays The Cole Porter Songbook", Sarah Vaughan's "I Get A Kick Out Of You: The Cole Porter Songbook, Volume 2", "The Herbie Hancock Quartet Live"

The Lady Is A Tramp - Published sheet music. "Presenting The Gerry Mulligan Sextet", Oscar Peterson's "The Song Is You", "Frank Sinatra Sings The Select Rodgers And Hart", Peggy Lee from the compilation "Isn't It Romantic: Capitol Sings Rodgers And Hart", "Gerry Mulligan Quartet", Ella Fitzgerald's "The Rodgers And Hart Songbook, Volume 1"

Lester Leaps In - "Count Basie At Newport", "The Best Of Lester Young", Charlie Parker's "The Legendary Rockland Palace Concert 1952, Vol. 1", "The Essential Count Basie, Volume 2"

Let's Call The Whole Thing Off - Published sheet music. Sarah Vaughan's "The George Gershwin Songbook, Volume 2", "Ella Fitzgerald Sings The George And Ira Gershwin Songbook", Ella Fitzgerald and Louis Armstrong's " 'S Wonderful - The Gershwin Songbook", Lynda Jamison's "You And The Night And The Music"

Let's Do It - Published sheet music. Louis Armstrong's "Night And Day: The Cole Porter Songbook", Ella Fitzgerald's "The Cole Porter Songbook, Volume 1", "Dick Hyman Plays The Great American Songbook", Trudy Richards' "Crazy In Love"

Li'l Darlin' - Published Neal Hefti big band arrangement. "The World Of Count Basie", Oscar Peterson's "Paris Jazz Concert"

A Lot Of Livin' To Do - Published sheet music. Lee Morgan's "Standards", Count Basie Orchestra's "Broadway Basie's Way", Buddy Greco's "Let's Love"

Love For Sale - Published sheet music. "Charlie Parker Plays Standards", "The Essential Billie Holiday", Miles Davis' "Black Giants", Jackie Terrasson's "Lover Man", "George Shearing And The Montgomery Brothers", Charlie Parker's "The Cole Porter Songbook", "Sonny Criss Plays Cole Porter", Oscar Peterson's "The Song Is You", Kenny Barron's "The Only One", Al Cohn and Zoot Sims' "Anything Goes: The Cole Porter Songbook", "Oscar Peterson Plays The Cole Porter Songbook", "Piano Bar By Erroll Garner", "The Charlie Parker Story, Volume 2", Ella Fitzgerald's "Dream Dancing", "Mel Torme And Friends", Shirley Horn's "Night And Day: The Cole Porter Songbook", "Frank Vignola - Appel Direct"

Love Is A Many Splendored Thing - Published sheet music. Keith Jarrett's "Standards In Norway"

Love Me Or Leave Me - Published sheet music. Miles Davis' "Walkin' ", "The Best Of Gerry Mulligan Quartet With Chet Baker", Coleman Hawkins and Pee Wee Russell's "Jam Session In Swingsville"

Love Speaks Louder Than Words - Composer's lead sheet. Al Jarreau's "High Crime"

Love Walked In - Published sheet music. "Ella Fitzgerald Sings The George And Ira Gershwin Songbook", George Shearing's "Jazz Concert", "George Shearing And The Montgomery Brothers", "The Incredible Kai Winding", Andre Previn's "We Got Rhythm - A Gershwin Songbook", Erroll Garner's "Magician/Gershwin And Kern", Sarah Vaughan's "The George Gershwin Songbook, Volume 1", Louis Armstrong's " 'S Wonderful - The Gershwin Songbook", Fred Hersch & Jack Jones' "The Gershwin Album", The Modern Jazz Quartet's "Concorde", "The Piano Style Of Nat King Cole"

Lover, Come Back To Me - Published sheet music. "Piano Bar By Erroll Garner", "The Essential Billie Holiday", Chris Conner's "Lover, Come Back To Me", "Cy Coleman Trio"

Lucky To Be Me - Published sheet music. Irene Kral's "Where Is Love?", "Everybody Digs Bill Evans", Kenny Burrell's "Sunup To Sundown", Dave McKenna's "Solo Piano"

Lullaby Of Broadway - Published sheet music. "Kenny Drew Plays The Music Of Harry Warren And Harold Arlen", Randy Sanke's "The Chase", Rosemary Clooney/Count Basie's "'At Long Last"

The Man I Love - Published sheet music. "Ella Fitzgerald Sings The George And Ira Gershwin Songbook", Sarah Vaughan's "The George Gershwin Songbook, Volume 2", Betty Carter's " 'S Wonderful - The Gershwin Songbook", Enrico Pieranunzi's "No Man's Land", Toshiko Akiyoshi's "The Many Sides Of Toshiko", "The Roy Eldrige Quintet", Ella Fitzgerald's "Ella In Berlin - Mack The Knife" and "Ella á Nice", Thelonious Monk's " The London Collection, Volume Three", Andre Previn's "We Got Rhythm - A Gershwin Songbook", "Buddy DeFranco And Oscar Peterson Play George Gershwin", Louis Smith from the compilation "Rhapsody In Blue: Blue Note Plays The Music Of George And Ira Gershwin", Coleman Hawkins and Lester Young's "Classic Tenors", "Dick Hyman Plays The Great American Songbook", "Concord All-Stars On Cape Cod", Eddie "Lockjaw" Davis' "Gentle Jaws"

The Man That Got Away - Published sheet music. Coleman Hawkins' "On Broadway", Ella Fitzgerald's "The Harold Arlen Songbook, Volume 2", Judy Garland from the compilation "Over The Rainbow - Capitol Sings Harold Arlen", Ruby Braff/Dick Hyman's "Manhattan Jazz"

Meditation - Published sheet music. "Francis Albert Sinatra And Antonio Carlos Jobim", João Gilberto's "The Girl From Ipanema: The Antonio Carlos Jobim Songbook"

Minute By Minute - Published sheet music. "Listen To The Music - The Very Best Of The Doobie Brothers"

Miss Otis Regrets - Published sheet music. Ella Fitzgerald's "The Cole Porter Songbook, Volume 1", Francis Faye's "No Reservations"

Moondance - Published sheet music. Van Morrison's "A Night In San Francisco", Georgie Fame's "Cool Cat Blues"

The More I See You - Published sheet music. Nat "King" Cole's "The Very Thought Of You", Cyrus Chestnut's "Nut", "Count Basie Big Band

Montreux '77", Dudley Moore's "Today"

Mountain Greenery - Published sheet music. "Mel Torme And Friends", Ella Fitzgerald's "The Rodgers And Hart Songbook, Volume 2", Barney Kessell's "Music To Listen To Barney Kessell By", Tony Bennett's "More Great Rodgers And Hart Songs", Bing Crosby's "Bings Sings Whilst Breman Swings"

Mr. Lucky - Published sheet music. Henry Mancini's "Music from 'Mr. Lucky' ", Donald Byrd's "Out Of This World", Bobby Hackett's "The Music Of Henry Mancini", Royce Campbell's "Tribute Mancini"

My Funny Valentine - Published sheet music. "My Funny Valentine: Miles Davis In Concert", Miles Davis' "Workin' ", Ben Webster's "Music For Loving", Ella Fitzgerald's "The Rodgers And Hart Songbook, Volume 2", "Frank Sinatra Sings The Select Rodgers And Hart", Keith Jarrett's "Still Live", Enrico Pieranunzi's "No Man's Land", Fred Hersch's "Dancing In The Dark", Ahmad Jamal's "Cross Country Tour: 1958-1961", Chet Baker's "My Funny Valentine", Sarah Vaughan's "All-Time Favorites", "New York Swing Tributes Rodgers And Hart", "Milt Jackson Quartet"

My Heart Stood Still - Published sheet music. "Piano Bar By Erroll Garner", Ella Fitzgerald's "The Rodgers And Hart Songbook, Volume 2", Bill Evans' "Peace Piece And Other Pieces", "Stan Getz And Bill Evans", Sarah Vaughan's "Great Songs From Hit Shows, Volume 2", "The Piano Styles Of Nat King Cole", "Chet Baker Sings: It Could Happen To You", "New York Swing Tributes Rodgers And Hart", Chris Conner's "Lover, Come Back To Me"

My Man's Gone Now - Published sheet music. Bill Evans' "Sunday At The Village Vanguard" and "The Secret Sessions", Miles Davis' "Porgy And Bess", Sarah Vaughan's "The George Gershwin Songbook, Volume 1", Dave Grusin's "The Gershwin Connection", Bill Evans and Jim Hall's "Intermodulation", Joe Henderson's "Porgy And Bess", "Carmen McRae", Shirley Horn's "I Remember Miles"

Nancy (With The Laughing Face) - Published sheet music. John Coltrane's "Ballads", Cannonball Adderley's "Know What I Mean?", Ben Webster's "The Jeep Is Jumpin' " and "Warm Moods", Paul Desmond's "Take Ten"

Nice Work If You Can Get It - Published sheet music. "Sarah Vaughan In Hi-Fi", "Ella Fitzgerald Sings The George And Ira Gershwin Songbook", Dave Grusin's "The Gershwin Collection", "Carmen McRae", "Stan Getz-Bob Brookmeyer Quintet", Ella Fitzgerald and Andre Previn's "Nice Work If You Can Get It", Erroll Garner's "Magician/Gershwin And Kern". Thelonious Monk from the compilation "Rhapsody In Blue: Blue Note Plays The Music Of George And Ira Gershwin", Billie Holiday "Velvet Moods", Marc Gasbarro's "Gershwin On Monarch: The Crown Project", Jack Jones' "The Gershwin Album", Mel Torme's "A Very Special Time"

Night And Day - Published sheet music. Charlie Parker's "The Cole Porter Songbook", Ella Fitzgerald's "The Cole Porter Songbook, Volume 2", Joe Henderson's "Inner Urge", "Everybody Digs Bill Evans", "Stan Getz And Bill Evans", "Oscar Peterson Plays Cole Porter", "Sonny Criss Plays Cole Porter", Coleman Hawkins' "The Complete Keynote Collection", "Dick Hyman Plays The Great American Songbook", "Frank Sinatra Sings The Select Cole Porter", Fred Astaire's "I Get A Kick Out Of You: The Cole Porter Songbook, Volume 2", Howard Alden and George Van Epps' "Seven And Seven"

Not Like This - Al Jarreau's "Jarreau", Rebecca Paris' "Spring", Mark Murphy's "I'll Close My Eyes", Helen Merril's "Clear Out Of This World"

Of Thee I Sing - Published sheet music. "Ella Fitzgerald Sings The George And Ira Gershwin Songbook", Sarah Vaughan's "The George Gershwin Songbook, Volume 1", "The Essential Stan Getz: The Getz Songbook"

Oh, Lady Be Good - Published sheet music. Red Garland's "Manteca", "Ella Fitzgerald Sings The George And Ira Gershwin Songbook", Charlie Parker's "Jazz At The Philharmonic 1946", "Piano Bar By Erroll Garner", "The Best Of Ella Fitzgerald", Andre Previn's "We Got Rhythm - A Gershwin Songbook", Joe Pass' "Blues For Fred", Benny Goodman's "Gershwin Standard Time", The Gordons with Dizzy Gillespie's " 'S Wonderful: The Gershwin Songbook", Fats Navarro/Tadd Dameron's "Royal Roost Sessions 1948", Benny Carter's "Frenesi", Joe Pass/Herb Ellis' "Two For The Road", Matt Catingub's "George Gershwin 100", Fred Astaire's " 'S Marvelous: The Gershwin Songbook"

The Old Country - Keith Jarrett's "Standards Live", "Nancy Wilson And Cannonball Adderley", Nat Adderley's "The Old Country", Joe Heinemann's "Just Joe"

Old Folks - Published sheet music. Miles Davis' "Someday My Prince Will Come", Keith Jarrett's "Standards In Norway", Kenny Burrell's "Lotus Blossom", "Steve Kuhn: Live At Maybeck Recital Hall, Volume 13", Astral Project's "Voodoo Bop"

On A Clear Day - Published sheet music. Cal Tjader and Eddie Palmieri's "El Sonido Nuevo", Joe Henderson's "Straight, No Chaser", Barney Kessel's "Autumn Leaves", George Shearing's "New Look", Oscar Peterson's "The Good Life"

On A Misty Night - Tadd Dameron's "The Magic Touch", Tadd Dameron and John Coltrane's "Mating Call", Warren Rand's "Dameron II-V", Andy Laverne's "Time Well Spent"

One Hundred Ways - Published sheet music. Quincy Jones' "The Dude", Dave Sanborn's "Straight To The Heart"

Our Delight - Dizzy Gillespie's "Shaw' 'Nuff", Tadd Dameron's "The Magic Touch", "The Fabulous Fats Navarro", Fats Navarro's "Royal Roost Sessions 1948", Phineas Newborn's "We Three"

(Our) Love Is Here To Stay - Published sheet music. "Ella Fitzgerald Sings The George And Ira Gershwin Songbook", "Bill Evans At Shelley's Manne-Hole", Harry "Sweets" Edison's "Sweets", "The Gene Ammons Story", The Modern Jazz Quartet's "Concorde", Shirley Horn's " 'S Wonderful: The Gershwin Songbook", Ben Webster's "See You At The Fair", "Gene Norman Presents Mel Torme", Blossom Dearie's "Once Upon A Summertime", Gene Kelly's "American Popular Song", "Introducing Jimmy Cleveland And His All-Stars", Andre Previn's "We Got Rhythm - A Gershwin Songbook", Brian Atkinson from the compilation "Gershwin On Monarch: The Crown Project"

People Make The World Go Round - "The Best Of The Stylistics"

Piano In The Dark - Published sheet music. Brenda Russell's "Greatest Hits"

Pick Up The Pieces - Published sheet music. Average White Band's "AWB"

Please Don't Talk About Me When I'm Gone - Published sheet music. Sonny Stitt/Paul Gonsalves' "Salt And Pepper", "Ruby Braff-Buddy Tate With The Newport All-Stars", Terrie Richards Alden's "Voice With Heart", Joe Williams' "In Good Company"

Put On A Happy Face - Published sheet music. Oscar Peterson's "Exclusively For My Friends - The Lost Tapes", Tal Farlow's "Sign Of The Times"

Real Love - Published sheet music. "Listen To The Music - The Very Best Of The Doobie Brothers"

Red Clay - Freddie Hubbard's "Red Clay", "Mark Murphy Sings"

Rockin' In Rhythm - Published big band arrangement. Duke Ellington's "Jazz After Dark" and "Piano In The Background" and "The Best Of Duke Ellington", Clare Fischer's "Rockin' In Rhythm", Hank Jones/Ray Brown/Jimmie Smith's "Rockin' In Rhythm", Cleo Laine's "Solitude", Hank Jones and Tommy Flanagan's "I'm All Smiles", Steve Lacy's "Soprano Sax", The Modern Jazz Quartet's "For Ellington", Bob Ferrel's "Time Tunnel"

'Round Midnight - Published sheet music. Miles Davis' " 'Round Midnight", "Thelonious Monk's Greatest Hits", "Thelonious Monk At The Blackhawk", Thelonious Monk's "Thelonious Himself", "Monkisms" and "Jazz Piano Anthology - Bop - Volume 2", Bill Evans' "Conversations With Myself", Art Pepper's "The Art Of The Ballad" and "Modern Jazz Classics", Cyrus Chestnut's "Nut", Stan Getz' "Cool Velvet", Lee Konitz, Brad Mehldau and Charlie Haden's "Alone Together", Sarah Vauhgan's "Essential Jazz Ballads"

'S Wonderful - Published sheet music. Red Garland's "Manteca", "Ella Fitzgerald Sings The George And Ira Gershwin Songbook", Sarah Vaughan's "The George Gershwin Songbook, Volume 1", Alan Broadbent's "Another Time", Andre Previn's "We Got Rhythm - A Gershwin Songbook", Lee Morgan from the compilation "Rhapsody In Blue: Blue Note Plays The Music Of George And Ira Gershwin", Joe Williams' " 'S Wonderful: The Gershwin Songbook", Coleman Hawkins' "Verve Jazz Masters 34", "Buddy DeFranco And Oscar Peterson Play George Gershwin", Suzannah McCorkle's "Someone To Watch Over Me", Don Elliott's " 'S Paradise: The Gershwin Songbook", Jack Jones' "The Gershwin Album"

Sabiá - Published sheet music. Antonio Carlos Jobim's "Stone Flower" and "Terra Brasilis", Cedar Walton's "The Maestro", Susannah McCorkle's "Sabia"

Saving All my Love For You - Published sheet music. "Whitney Houston"

Secret Love - Published sheet music. Fred Hersch's "Dancing In The Dark", Vincent Herring's "Secret Love", Peter Nero's "Young And Warm And Wonderful"

September In The Rain - Published sheet music. Red Garland's "A Garland Of Red", "The Complete Capitol Live Recordings Of George Shearing", "Kenny Drew Plays The Music Of Harry Warren And Harold Arlen"

Serenade In Blue - Published sheet music. Eddie "Lockjaw" Davis' "Gentle Jaws", "Kenny Drew Plays The Music Of Harry Warren And Harold Arlen", "The Essential Stan Getz: The Getz Songbook", Oscar Peterson's "The Song Is You", Gloria Lynne's "Golden Classics", Dexter Gordon's "Landslide"

Shiny Stockings - Published sheet music. Count Basie's "April In Paris", Ella Fitzgerald's "Compact Jazz"

Since I Fell For You - Published sheet music. Ella Fitzgerald's "Lady Time", Jimmy Smith's "Home Cookin' ", "The Complete Dinah Washington On Mercury, Volume 2", Stanley Turrentine's "Blue Hour", "Have You Met Inez Jones?", Morning and Jim Nichols' "My Flame"

Slow Hot Wind - Published sheet music. "Sarah Vaughan Sings The Henry Mancini Songbook", Johnny Hartman's "The Voice That Is", "Monica Mancini", Ray Obiedo's "Modern World", "Sandy Graham"

So In Love - Published sheet music. "Chick Corea Akoustic Band", Walter Norris' "Sunburst", Fred Hersch's "Dancing In The Dark", Ella Fitzgerald's "The Cole Porter Songbook, Volume 1", Randy Sanke's "The Chase", Dinah Washington's "I Get A Kick Out Of You: The Cole Porter Songbook, Volume 1", John Raitt's "Highlight Of Broadway"

So Nice (Summer Samba) - Published sheet music. Astrud Gilberto's "A Certain Smile, A Certain Sadness", Johnny Mathis' "The Global Masters",

Softly, As In A Morning Sunrise - Published sheet music. John Coltrane's "Live At The Village Vanguard", Alan Broadbent's "Everything I Love", Wynton Kelly's "Kelly Blue", Roseanna Vitro's "Softly"

Some Other Time - Published sheet music. Bill Evans' "Waltz For Debby"

Somebody Loves Me - Published sheet music. Sonny Clark's "Blues In The Night", "Oscar Peterson Plays Gershwin", "Ella Fitzgerald Sings The George And Ira Gershwin Songbook", "Dick Hyman Plays The Great American Songbook", Mark Garbarro from the compilation "Gershwin On Monarch: The Crown Project", Peggy Lee's "Songs From 'Pete Kelly's Blues' ", Bing Crosby's "Gershwin Standard Time"

Someone To Watch Over Me - Published sheet music. Chet Baker's "My Funny Valentine", Chick Corea's "Expressions", "Chet Baker Sings", Frank Sinatra's "Songs For Young Lovers", Morgana King's "Stardust", Coleman Hawkins from the compilation "Rhapsody In Blue: Blue Note Plays The Music Of George Gershwin", Erroll Garner's "Magician/Gershwin And Kern", "Buddy DeFranco And Oscar Peterson Play George Gershwin", George Cables' "By George", Andre Previn's "We Got Rhythm - A Gershwin Songbook", Sandi Patti from the compilation "Gershwin On Monarch: The Crown Project", "Lee Wiley Sings The Songs Of Ira And George Gershwin", Jack Jones' "The Gershwin Album"

Something To Talk About - Bonnie Raitt's "Luck Of The Draw"

Sometimes I'm Happy - Published sheet music. "Piano Bar By Erroll Garner", "Four Freshman And Five Saxes", Tony Bennett's "American Popular Song"

A Song For You - "Leon Russell"

Soon - Published sheet music. "More Ella Fitzgerald", "Ella Fitzgerald Sings The George And Ira Gershwin Songbook", Sarah Vaughan's "The George Gershwin Songbook, Volume 1", Dave Grusin's "The Gershwin Connection", Jack Jones' "The Gershwin Album", Gary Burton's "Like Minds", Andre Previn's "We Got Rhythm - A Gershwin Songbook", Connie Boswell from the compilation " 'S Wonderful: The Great Decca Gershwin Songbook"

Soul Man - Sam and Dave from the compilation "50 Years: Atlantic Records - The Gold Anniversary Collection"

Stormy Weather - Published sheet music. Joe Pass' "Songs For Helen", Lena Horne's "American Popular Song", Andre Previn's "Uptown", Keely Smith from the compilation "Over The Rainbow: Capitol Sings Harold Arlen"

Strike Up The Band - Published sheet music. "Oscar Peterson Plays Gershwin", Erroll Garner's "Magician/ Gershwin And Kern", Bob Cooper from the compilation "Rhapsody In Blue: Blue Note Plays The Music Of George And Ira Gershwin", "Dick Hyman Plays The Great American Songbook", "Ella Fitzgerald Sings The George And Ira Gershwin Songbook", Ray Charles' "Genius + Soul = Jazz", Tony Bennett and Count Basie's "Gershwin Standard Time", Sonny Stitt/Bud Powell/J.J.Johnson's "I Want To Be Happy"

Stuck On You - Published sheet music. Lionel Richie's "Can't Slow Down"

Suite Judy Blue Eyes - Published sheet music. "Crosby, Stills And Nash"

The Summer Knows - Published sheet music. Bill Evans' "Montreux III", Art Farmer's "Ambrosia", "Art Pepper"

Summer Night - Published sheet music. Keith Jarrett's "Bye Bye Blackbird", Miles Davis' "Quiet Nights", Alan Broadbent's "Pacific Standard Time", Roy Haynes' "When It's Haynes, It Roars", Hal Galper's "Invitation To A Concert"

Summertime - Published sheet music. Miles Davis' "Porgy And Bess", Joe Henderson's "Porgy And Bess", "Chet Baker In Paris, Volume 2", Stan Getz' "Nobody Else But Me", Sarah Vaughan's "The George Gershwin Songbook", Art Blakey's "A Jazz Message", George Cables' "By George", Andre Previn's "We Got Rhythm - A Gershwin Songbook", Susannah McCorkle's "Someone To Watch Over Me", Hank Jones from the compilation "Rhapsody In Blue: Blue Notes Plays The Music Of George Gershwin", "Ella Fitzgerald Sings The George And Ira Gershwin Songbook", Helen Merrill's " 'S Wonderful: The Gershwin Songbook", Erroll Garner's "Body And Soul"

Sunny - Published sheet music. Bobby Hebb from the compilation, "45s On CD, Volume 3 (1966)", Wes Montgomery's "California Dreamin' ", Pat Martino's "Live"

Sure Enough - Publisher's lead sheet. Tom Scott's "Desire"

Sweet Georgia Brown - Published sheet music. "An Evening With Herb Ellis", Charlie Parker's "Jazz At The Philharmonic 1946", "The Best Of Bud Powell On Verve", Andre Previn's "Old Friends", Dave McKenna's "Solo Piano", Diane Schur's "In Tribute"

Take Five - Published sheet music. Dave Brubeck's "Time Out", Carmen McRae and Dave Brubeck's "Take Five"

Takin' It To The Streets - Published sheet music. "Listen To The Music - The Very Best Of The Doobie Brothers"

Tea For Two - Published sheet music. "Art Tatum Trio: Members Edition", Thelonious Monk's "The Art Of The Ballad", "The Best Of Bud Powell On Verve", Hank Jones' "Urbanity", Ella Fitzgerald's "Pure Ella", "The Piano Style Of Nat King Cole", Oscar Peterson's "The Song Is You", Coleman Hawkins and Roy Eldridge's "At The Opera House", "John Colianni At Maybeck"

Teach Me Tonight - Published sheet music. Erroll Garner's "Concerts By The Sea", "Compact Jazz: Count Basie And Joe Williams", Birelli Langrene's "Standards", Buddy Greco's "Let's Love"

That Certain Feeling - Published sheet music. "Ella Fitzgerald Sings The George And Ira Gershwin Songbook", George Gershwin on Dave Grusin's "The Gershwin Connection", Josephine Baker's "Breezin' Along", "Bobby Short Is K-R-A-Z-Y For Gershwin", Felicia Sanders from the compilation " 'S Wonderful - The Great Gershwin Decca Songbook"

That Sunday, That Summer - Published sheet music. Natalie Cole's "Unforgettable - With Love", "Dinah Washington: The Best Of The Roulette Years", Ernestine Anderson's "Boogie Down", Betty Carter's "Look What I Got"

That's What Friends Are For - Published sheet music. "Dionne Warwick/Greatest Hits 1979-1990"

Then I'll Be Tired Of You - Published sheet music. John Coltrane's "Stardust", Ahmad Jamal's "Rhapsody", "At Ease With Coleman Hawkins", Mel Torme & George Shearing's "An Evening At Charlie's"

There's A Small Hotel - Published sheet music. "Chet Baker In Paris, Volume 2", Charlie Parker's "An Evening At Home With The Bird", Ella Fitzgerald's "The Rodgers And Hart Songbook", "Stan Getz Quartets", "Oscar Peterson Plays Pretty", Billy Eckstein's "Broadway, Bongos And Mr. B", "Bobby Short Celebrates Rodgers And Hart"

There's No You - Published sheet music. Mark Murphy's "Kerouac, Then And Now", "The Great Ray Charles", "Louis Armstrong Meets Oscar Peterson", Ben Webster's "Warm Moods", Ella Fitzgerald & Joe Pass' "Speak Love"

They All Laughed - Published sheet music. George Shearing's "Touch Of Genius", Ella Fitzgerald and Louis Armstrong's "Ella And Louis Again", Andre Previn's "We Got Rhythm - A Gershwin Songbook", Susannah McCorkle's "Someone To Watch Over Me", Bing Crosby's "Bing Sings Whilst Bregman Swings"

They Can't Take That Away From Me - Published sheet music. "Ella Fitzgerald Sings The George And Ira Gershwin Songbook", Sarah Vaughan's "The George Gershwin Songbook", Billie Holiday's " 'S Wonderful: The Gershwin Songbook", Ella Fitzgerald and Louis Armstrong's "Ella And Louis", Joe Pass' "Blues For Fred", Diana Kral's "Love Scenes", Erroll Garner's "Concerts By The Sea", "Cy Coleman Trio", Tim Davis from the compilation "Gershwin On Monarch: The Crown Project", "Buddy DeFranco And Oscar Peterson Play George Gershwin", Julie London from the compilation, "Rhapsody In Blue: Blue Note Plays The Music Of George Gershwin", Matt Catingub's "George Gershwin 100", Susannah McCorkle's "Someone To Watch Over Me", "The Fred Astaire Story"

This Heart Of Mine - Published sheet music. Fred Hersch's "Sarabande", Freddie Cole's "Live At Birdland West", Warren Vaché's "Warren Plays Warren"

This Is Always - Published sheet music. Irene Kral's "Better Than Anything", "Chet Baker Sings", The Gene Ammons Story", Concord All-Stars On Cape Cod"

Those Eyes - Kenny Rankin's "Here In My Heart", Rosa Passos' "Pano Pra Manga"

Thou Swell - Published sheet music. "Horace Silver Trio", Ella Fitzgerald's "The Cole Porter Songbook, Volume 2", Joe Williams' "The Greatest", Benny Carter's "Swingin' The '20s", "Compact Jazz: Count Basie And Joe Williams", Margaret Whiting from the compilation "Isn't It Romantic - Capitol Sings Rodgers And Hart", "New York Swing Tributes Rodgers And Hart"

Through The Fire - Chaka Khan's "I Feel For You"

Time After Time - Published sheet music. John Coltrane's "Stardust", George Shearing's "Compact Jazz", Ben Webster's "Warm Moods", Bobbe Norris' "You And The Night And The Music", "The Ralph Sharon Trio Swings The Sammy Cahn Songbook", Matt Monroe from the compilation "It's Magic: Capitol Sings Sammy Cahn", "Concord All-Stars On Cape Cod"

A Time For Love - Published sheet music. Bill Evans' "Alone", Stan Getz' "The Dolphin", "Sue Raney Sings The Music Of Johnny Mandel", Bill Watrous' "A Time For Love"

Time On My Hands - Published sheet music. "Sonny Rollins", Chet Baker's "Chet", Art Farmer's "Soul Eyes", Gene Ammons and Sonny Stitt's "We'll Be Together Again", Coleman Hawkins' "Verve Jazz Masters 34", Coleman Hawkins and Roy Eldridge's "At The Opera House", Ahmad Jamal's "Cross Country Tour 1958-1961", "The Legendary Lee Wiley"

'Tis Autumn - Published sheet music. Bob Dorough's "Just About Everything", "Joe Williams And Friends", Chet Baker's "Chet", Red Garland's "All Kinds Of Weather"

Tokyo Blues - Composer's lead sheet. Horace Silver's "Tokyo Blues"

Too Marvelous For Words - Published sheet music. "Ella Fitzgerald Sings The Johnny Mercer Songbook", Jackie & Roy's "High Standards", Frank Sinatra's "Sinatra And The Sextet: Live In Paris" and "Songs For Swingin' Lovers", "Dream: Johnny Costa Plays Johnny Mercer"

Too Much Saké - Composer's lead sheet. Horace Silver's "Tokyo Blues"

Trouble Is A Man - Sarah Vaughan's "Trouble Is A Man", Bobbe Norris' "You And The Night And The Music", "At Ease With Coleman Hawkins", Milt Jackson's "Feelings"

Twilight World - Published sheet music. Marian McPartland's "Just Friends" and "Silent Pool"

Two For The Road - Published sheet music. Dave Grusin's "Two For The Road", Henry Mancini's "Two For The Road: Soundtrack", Charlie Byrd's "The Music Of Henry Mancini", Dudley Moore's "Today"

The Underdog - Published sheet music. Dave Frishberg's "Let's Eat Home"

Until It's Time For You To Go - Published sheet music. Roberta Flack's "Chapter Two", Frank Morgan's "Lament", Ray Bryant's "Alone At Montreux", Cleo Laine's "A Beautiful Thing"

Until The Real Thing Comes Along - Published sheet music. Dexter Gordon's "A Swinging Affair", Carmen McRae's "Fine And Mellow", Coleman Hawkins' "In A Mellow Tone", June Christy's "Something Cool"

Valdez In The Country - George Benson's "In Flight", Donny Hathaway's "Extensions Of A Man"

Walk On By - Published sheet music. Stan Getz' "What The World Needs Now", Dionne Warwick's "Dionne Sings Dionne" and "Walk On By", Roland Kirk's "Slightly Latin", "Cal Tjader Sounds Out Burt Bacharach", Wynton Kelly's "Full View", Stanley Turrentine's "Blue Bacharach: A Cooler Shaker"

Walkin' - Miles Davis' "Walkin' ", "Friday Night At The Blackhawk", "The Complete Live Recordings At The Plugged Nickel-1965" and "Four And More", J.J. Johnson & Nat Adderley's "The Yokohama Concert", The Double Six Of Paris' "Les Double Six", "The Gene Ammons Story"

We're In This Love Together - Published sheet music. Al Jarreau's "Breakin' Away"

What A Fool Believes - Published sheet music. "Listen To The Music: The Very Best Of The Doobie Brothers"

What Am I Here For? - Duke Ellington's "Piano In The Background", "Stomp, Look And Listen" and "Fargo, ND, November 7, 1940", Count Basie's "April In Paris", "Clifford Brown And Max Roach", Andre Previn's "After Hours", "Duke Ellington"

What Is This Thing Called Love? - Published sheet music. Bill Evans' "Portrait In Jazz", "The Cannonball Adderley Quintet Live At The Lighthouse", Red Garland's "A Garland Of Red", "Charlie Parker Plays Standards", Charlie Parker's "The Cole Porter Songbook", "Sonny Criss Plays Cole Porter", Ahmad Jamal's "Cross Country Tour 1958-1961", "Frank Sinatra Sings The Select Cole Porter", Ella Fitzgerald's "The Cole Porter Songbook, Volume 2", "Billie Holiday's Greatest Hits", Oscar Peterson's "The Song Is You", Mel Torme's "Night And Day: The Cole Porter Songbook", Fred Hersch's "Sarabande", Joe Henderson's "Straight, No Chaser", Keely Smith's "Swingin' Pretty", Lee Konitz/Brad Mehldau/Charlie Haden's "Alone Together", Grant Green's "The Complete Quartets With Sonny Clark"

What The World Need Now Is Love - Published sheet music. Stan Getz' "What The World Needs Now", McCoy Tyner's "The Music Of Burt Bacharach", Stanley Turrentine's "Blue Bacharach", Dionne Warwick's "Dionne Sings Dionne", Mulgrew Miller's "The Countdown"

Wheelers And Dealers - Composer's lead sheet. Irene Kral's "Kral Space", Dave Frishberg's "The Dave Frishberg Songbook, Volume 2"

When A Man Loves A Woman - Published sheet music. "Percy Sledge's Greatest Hits", Wes Montgomery's "Greatest Hits"

When The World Was Young - Published sheet music. Stan Getz' "Paris Concert", "Mel Torme And Friends", Kenny Burrell's "Lotus Blossom", June Christy's "Gone For The Day"

When Your Lover Has Gone - Published sheet music. "The Essential Billie Holiday", Sonny Rollins' "Tenor Madness", Eddie "Lockjaw" Davis' "Gentle Jaws", "John Colianni At Maybeck", Linda Ronstadt's "Lush Life"

Where Or When - Published sheet music. "Clifford Brown With Strings", Ella Fitzgerald's "The Rodgers And Hart Songbook, Volume 1", "Frank Sinatra Sings The Select Rodgers And Hart", Erroll Garner's "The Nearness Of You" and "Concerts By The Sea", Gene Ammons' "Jugs And Dodo", "Bobby Short Celebrates Rodgers And Hart"

Who Cares? - Published sheet music. Cannonball Adderley's "Know What I Mean?", "Ella Fitzgerald Sings The George And Ira Gershwin Songbook", Anita O'Day's "Of Thee I Sing", Art Farmer's "Art", "Dick Hyman Plays The Great American Songbook", Susannah McCorkle's "Someone To Watch Over Me", Jack Jones' "The Gershwin Album"

Why Try To Change Me Now? - Published sheet music. Frank Sinatra's "I've Got A Crush On You", Nancy Wilson's "Welcome To My World", Arnett Cobb with The Red Garland Trio's "Blue And Sentimental", Roseanna Vitro's "Softly"

With A Song In My Heart - Published sheet music. Bill Evans' "Empathy", "Sonny Rollins", Ella Fitzgerald's "The Rodgers And Hart Songbook, Volume 1", Mal Waldron's "Impressions", "Bobby Short Celebrates Rodgers And Hart"

You And The Night And The Music - Published sheet music. Bill Evans' "Green Dolphin Street", Bobbe Norris' "You And The Night And The Music", Chet Baker's "Chet", Keith Jarrett's "At The Deer Head Inn", Alan Broadbent's "Everything I Love", Jim Snidero's "Standards Plus", Renee Rosnes' "Without Words", Dave McKenna's "Dancing In The Dark"

You Are There - Published sheet music. "The Dave Frishberg Songbook, Volume 2", "Sue Raney Sings The Music Of Johnny Mandel"

You Are Too Beautiful - Published sheet music. "John Coltrane And Johnny Hartman", "Sonny Rollins At Music Inn", "Cannonball Adderley And Strings: Jump For Joy", "Ed Bickert And Don Thompson", "New York Swing Tributes Rodgers And Hart"

You Do Something To Me - Published sheet music. Ella Fitzgerald's "Ella á Nice" and "The Cole Porter Songbook, Volume 2", "Frank Sinatra Sings The Select Cole Porter", Jessica Williams' "Momentum", Larry Goldings' "Awareness"

You Go To My Head - Published sheet music. Billie Holiday's "American Popular Song", Mark Murphy's "Song For The Geese", "Clifford Brown Memorial Album", "Bud Powell: Complete Blue Note And Roost Recordings", Coleman Hawkins' "I Love You: Giants Of Jazz", "Louis Armstrong Meets Oscar Peterson", Mary Stallings' "Manhattan Moods"

You Make Me Feel Brand New - "The Best Of The Stylistics"

You Make Me Feel So Young - Published sheet music. "Chet Baker Sings: It Could Happen To You", Gene Harris' "Like A Lover", Frank Sinatra's "Duets" and "Song For Swingin' Lovers", Patrick Williams' "Sinatraland"

You Taught My Heart To Sing - Published sheet music. McCoy Tyner's "Reflections", Dianne Reeves' "I Remember"

You Took Advantage Of Me - Published sheet music. Ella Fitzgerald's "The Rodgers And Hart Songbook, Volume 1", Billie Holiday's "The Last Recording", Benny Carter's "Frenesi", Art Tatum's "20th Century Piano Genius", "Bobby Short Celebrates Rodgers And Hart", June Christy from the compilation "Isn't It Romantic: Capitol Sings Rodgers And Hart", Linda Ronstadt's "Lush Life", "Cy Coleman Trio", "New York Swing Tributes Rodgers And Hart"

You'd Be So Nice To Come Home To - Published sheet music. "Art Pepper Meets The Rhythm Section", McCoy Tyner's "Today And Tomorrow", "An Evening With George Shearing And Mel Torme", Bud Powell's "Complete Blue Note Recordings", "Frank Sinatra Sings The Select Cole Porter", Ben Webster and Coleman Hawkins from the compilation "Anything Goes: The Cole Porter Songbook, Instrumentals", Helen Merrill from Clifford Brown's "Jazz 'Round Midnight"

You'll Never Know - Published sheet music. Red Garland's "Bright And Breezy", "Kenny Drew Plays The Music Of Harry Warren And Harold Arlen", Bobby Darin from the compilation "An Affair To Remember: Capitol Sings Harry Warren, Volume 18"

You're The Top - Published sheet music. Ella Fitzgerald's "The Cole Porter Songbook, Volume 2", Louis Armstrong's "I Get A Kick Out Of You: The Cole Porter Songbook, Volume 2", Jean Turner's "From The Creative World Of Stan Kenton"

Yours Is My Heart Alone - Published sheet music. "Cannonball Adderly And The Poll-Winners", Ray Brown Trio's "Summertime", Oscar Peterson's "Last Call At The Blue Note", "The Gene Harris Trio Plus One", Jean Ronne's "Daydream"

SHER MUSIC CO. - The World's Premier Jazz & Latin Music Book Publisher!

(all method books also available in digital form at www.Shermusic.com)

BEST-SELLING BOOKS BY MARK LEVINE
The Jazz Theory Book
The Jazz Piano Book
Jazz Piano Masterclass: The Drop 2 Book
How to Voice Standards at the Piano

THE WORLD'S BEST FAKE BOOKS
The New Real Book - Vol.1 - C, Bb and Eb
The New Real Book - Vol.2 - C, Bb and Eb
The New Real Book - Vol.3 - C, Bb, Eb and Bass Clef
The Real Easy Book - Vol.1 - C, Bb, Eb and Bass Clef
    (Three-Horn Edition)
The Real Easy Book - Vol.2 - C, Bb, Eb and Bass Clef
The Real Easy Book - Vol.3 - C, Bb, Eb and Bass Clef
The Latin Real Easy Book - C, Bb, Eb and Bass Clef
The Standards Real Book - C, Bb and Eb
The Latin Real Book - C, Bb and Eb
The Real Cool Book - 14 West Coast 'Cool' Jazz Octet Charts
The All-Jazz Real Book - C, Bb and Eb
The European Real Book - C, Bb and Eb
The Best of Sher Music Real Books - C, Bb and Eb
The World's Greatest Fake Book - C version only
The Yellowjackets Songbook - (all parts)
The Latin Real Book - C, Bb and Eb

DIGITAL FAKE BOOKS (at shermusic.com only)
The New Real Book - Vol.1 - C, Bb and Eb
The Digital Standards Songbook
The Digital Real Book

LATIN MUSIC BOOKS
Decoding Afro-Cuban Jazz: The Music of Chucho Valdés
    and Irakere - by Chucho Valdés and Rebeca Mauleón
The Salsa Guidebook - by Rebeca Mauleón
The Latin Real Easy Book - C, Bb, Eb and Bass Clef
The Latin Bass Book - by Oscar Stagnaro and Chuck Sher
The True Cuban Bass - by Carlos del Puerto and Silvio Vergara
The Brazilian Guitar Book - by Nelson Faria
Inside the Brazilian Rhythm Section - Nelon Faria/Cliff Korman
The Conga Drummer's Guidebook - by Michael Spiro
Language of the Masters - by Michael Spiro
Introduction to the Conga Drum DVD - by Michael Spiro
Afro-Caribbean Grooves for Drumset - by Jean-Philippe Fanfant
Afro-Peruvian Percussion Ensemble - by Hector Morales
Flamenco Improvisation, Vol. 1-3 - by Enrique Vargas
(Bilingual)
The Latin Real Book - C, Bb and Eb
101 Montunos - by Rebeca Mauleón
Muy Caliente! - Afro-Cuban Book Play-Along CD
(Libros en Español)
El Libro del Jazz Piano - by Mark Levine
Teoria del Jazz - by Mark Levine (digital only)

JAZZ METHOD BOOKS
BASS
The Improvisor's Bass Method - by Chuck Sher
Concepts for Bass Soloing - by Marc Johnson & Chuck Sher
Walking Bassics - by Ed Fuqua
Foundation Exercises for Bass - by Chuck Sher

GUITAR
Jazz Guitar Voicings: The Drop 2 Book - by Randy Vincent
Three-Note Voicings and Beyond - by Randy Vincent
Line Games - by Randy Vincent
Jazz Guitar Soloing: The Cellular Approach - by Randy Vincent
The Guitarist's Introduction to Jazz - by Randy Vincent

PIANO
Playing for Singers - by Mike Greensill
An Approach to Comping: The Essentials - by Jeb Patton
An Approach to Comping, Vol.2: Advanced - by Jeb Patton
Wisdom of the Hand - by Marius Nordal

OTHER INSTRUMENTS
Inner Drumming - by George Marsh
Method for Chromatic Harmonica - by Max de Aloe
Modern Etudes for Solo Trumpet - by Cameron Pearce
New Orleans Trumpet - by Jim Thornton

FOR ALL INSTRUMENTS
The Jazz Harmony Book - by David Berkman
The Jazz Musician's Guide to Creative Practicing - D. Berkman
The Jazz Singer's Guidebook - by David Berkman
Metaphors for the Musician - Randy Halberstadt
Forward Motion - by Hal Galper
The Serious Jazz Practice Book - by Barry Finnerty
The Serious Jazz Book II - by Barry Finnerty
Building Solo Lines From Cells - by Randy Vincent
The Real Easy Ear Training Book - by Roberta Radley
Reading, Writing and Rhythmetic - by Roberta Radley
Minor is Major - by Dan Greenblatt
Jazz Scores and Analysis - Vol.1 - by Rick Lawn
Essential Grooves - by Moretti, Nicholl and Stagnaro
The Jazz Solos of Chick Corea - transcribed by Peter Sprague

FOR STUDENT MUSICIANS
The Blues Scales - by Dan Greenblatt - C, Bb and Eb
Rhythm First! - by Tom Kamp - C, Bb, Eb and Bass Clef
The Guitarist's Introduction to Jazz - by Randy Vincent
Jazz Songs for Student Violinists - by Keefe and Mitchell

CDs
Poetry+Jazz: A Magical Marriage
The New Real Book Play-Along CDs (for Vol.1) - #1, 2 and 3
The Latin Real Book Sampler CD
The Music of Charles Stevens

For more info, see www.shermusic.com